OCCASIONAL PAPER 227

D1794943

U.S. Fiscal Policies and Priorities for Long-Run Sustainability

Martin Mühleisen and Christopher Towe, Editors

with
Roberto Cardarelli
Paula De Masi
Iryna Ivaschenko
Michael Kell
Ayhan Kose
Jim Prust
Dominique Simard

INTERNATIONAL MONETARY FUND
Washington DC
2004

Production: IMF Multimedia Services Division
Composition: Julio R. Prego
Figures: Theodore F. Peters, Jr.

Cataloging-in-Publication Data

U.S. Fiscal Policies and Priorities for Long-Run Sustainability / Martin
    Mühleisen and Christopher Towe, editors; with Roberto Cardarelli . . . [et
    al.]—Washington, D.C.: International Monetary Fund, 2004.

      p. cm. — (Occasional paper / International Monetary Fund; 227)

    ISBN 1-58906-295-7

    Includes bibliographical references.

    1. Fiscal policy — United States 2. Budget — United States. 3. Social
security — United States. 4. Energy policy — United States. I. Mühleisen,
Martin. II. Towe, Christopher M., 1957– III. Cadarelli, R. (Roberto)
IV. Series: Occasional paper (International Monetary Fund); no. 227

HJ2381.U8 2004

recycled paper

Contents

The following symbols have been used throughout this paper:

. . . to indicate that data are not available;

— to indicate that the figure is zero or less than half the final digit shown, or that the item does not exist;

– between years or months (e.g., 2001–02 or January–June) to indicate the years or months covered, including the beginning and ending years or months.

"n.a." means not applicable.

"Billion" means a thousand million.

Minor discrepancies between constituent figures and totals are due to rounding.

The term "country," as used in this paper, does not in all cases refer to a territorial entity that is a state as understood by international law and practice; the term also covers some territorial entities that are not states, but for which statistical data are maintained and provided internationally on a separate and independent basis.

Preface

This paper presents an overview of recent U.S. fiscal developments and discusses possible implications of the sharp turnaround in the government's fiscal position. Against this background, it also reviews key policy challenges that will need to be addressed to cope with the mounting pressures on public retirement and health care systems during the next decade. *U.S. Fiscal Policies and Priorities for Long-Run Sustainability* draws principally on background papers that were prepared for the IMF staff's annual consultation discussions with the U.S. authorities in 2002 and 2003. Charles Collyns, Deputy Director of the Western Hemisphere Department, led the staff team and provided considerable guidance in compiling this volume. Anoop Singh, Director of the Western Hemisphere Department, also actively participated in the consultation discussions and directed the staff's background work.

The authors would like to thank the U.S. authorities for their cooperation and support during the policy discussions and technical meetings. They are indebted to Gustavo Ramirez and Victor Culiuc for first-rate research assistance and to Asegedech WoldeMariam for her excellent contribution to Section V. The authors are especially grateful to Alfred S. Go, Modupeh B. Williams, Joan F. McLeod-Tillman, and Mary Kelley for coordination and general assistance and to Archana Kumar of the External Relations Department for editing the paper and coordinating its production.

The opinions expressed are solely those of the authors and do not necessarily reflect the views of the International Monetary Fund, the Executive Directors, or the U.S. authorities.

Except where otherwise indicated, the paper reflects information available through end–September 2003.

I Overview: Returning Deficits and the Need for Fiscal Reform

Martin Mühleisen

U.S. government finances have experienced a remarkable turnaround in recent years. Within only a few years, hard-won gains of the previous decade have been lost and, instead of budget surpluses, deficits are again projected as far as the eye can see. The deterioration has not been restricted to the federal budget but has also taken place at the state and local government levels. As a result, the U.S. general government deficit is now among the highest in the industrialized world, and public debt levels are approaching those in other major industrial countries (Figure 1.1).

Although fiscal policies have undoubtedly provided valuable support to the recovery so far, the return to large deficits raises two interrelated concerns. First, with budget projections showing large federal fiscal deficits over the next decade, the recent emphasis on cutting taxes, boosting defense and security outlays, and spurring an economic recovery may come at the eventual cost of upward pressure on interest rates, a crowding out of private investment, and an erosion of longer-term U.S. productivity growth.

Second, the evaporation of fiscal surpluses has left the budget even less well prepared to cope with the retirement of the baby boom generation, which will begin later this decade and place massive pressure on the Social Security and Medicare systems. Without the cushion provided by earlier surpluses, there is less time to address these programs' underlying insolvency before government deficits and debt begin to increase unsustainably, making more urgent the need for meaningful reform.

The remainder of this section summarizes the IMF staff's assessment of the U.S. fiscal situation, describing both the factors that have contributed to the burgeoning of the deficit and the key policy challenges posed by the impending demographic transition. It ties together subsequent sections on domestic and international implications of current budget policies; long-term prospects for Social Security and Medicare; an intergenerational analysis of long-term fiscal imbalances; the role of energy taxation; effectiveness of spending rules; and state and local government finances.

The Fiscal Deficit: Back to Square One

The 1990s were marked by significant fiscal consolidation as the economy emerged from the 1991 recession and experienced one of the longest expansions in recent history. As a result, following many years of failed attempts at exerting fiscal discipline,

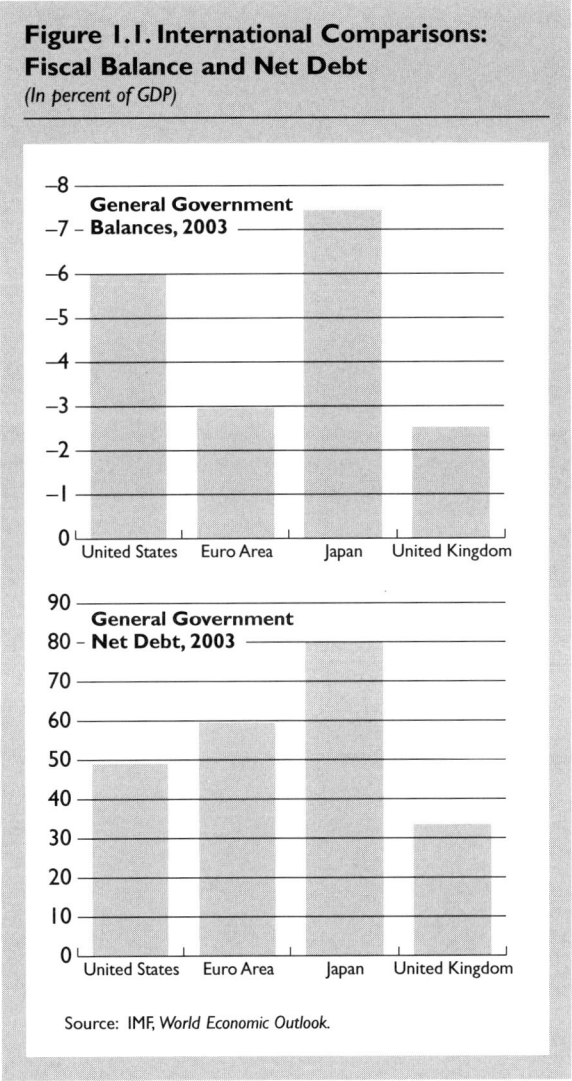

Figure 1.1. International Comparisons: Fiscal Balance and Net Debt
(In percent of GDP)

Source: IMF, *World Economic Outlook*.

Figure 1.2. Federal Budget Balance Adjusted for Cyclical Factors and Capital Gains Taxes
(In percent of potential GDP)

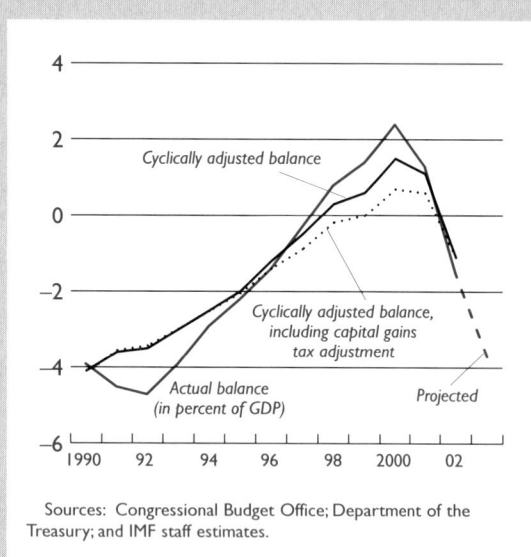

Sources: Congressional Budget Office; Department of the Treasury; and IMF staff estimates.

the federal budget—including the Social Security surplus—moved from a deficit of 4½ percent of GDP to surpluses that reached 2½ percent of GDP in FY2000 (Figure 1.2).[1]

Both macroeconomic developments and policy actions played an important role in achieving this correction. Strong economic growth buoyed tax revenues, and the stock market boom fueled an unprecedented increase in capital gains taxes. Estimates by the Congressional Budget Office (CBO, 2003) suggest that cyclical factors accounted for about 1 percent of GDP of the fiscal improvement between FY1992 and FY2000, just over half the shift in the deficit ratio (see Figure 1.2).[2] The balance was achieved through tax increases—including those incorporated in the 1993 Omnibus Budget Reconciliation Act—and the discipline over both mandatory and discretionary spending exerted by the 1990 Budget Enforcement Act.[3]

Since FY2000, however, the fiscal position has eroded rapidly and, with the deficit expected to exceed 4 percent of GDP in FY2004, essentially all the gains achieved during the earlier decade have disappeared. Again, as Table 1.1 shows, the reasons for this shift include both cyclical and policy factors:[4]

- The 2001 recession and the relatively weak recovery accounted for about half of the budgetary turnaround in FY2002 and FY2003. Sluggish employment growth weighed on personal income tax collections and boosted payments for income support and related programs. In addition, the bursting of the equity bubble sparked a substantial drop in capital gains tax collections, as shown in Figure 1.2, fully reversing the extraordinary increases in collections that had been achieved during the 1990s.

- On the policy front, expenditure discipline had already relaxed considerably in the face of prolonged budget surpluses. However, the September 11 attacks and the ensuing war on terrorism, as well as efforts to stimulate the economy, prompted major increases in outlays for defense and homeland security, as well as other programs (Figure 1.3). Altogether, discretionary spending increased from 6¼ percent of GDP in FY2000 to an expected 7¼ percent of GDP in FY2003, accounting for about one-fourth of the overall fiscal turnaround.[5]

- The remaining one-fourth of the turnaround resulted from tax cuts, which were enacted both to provide a countercyclical boost to the economy and bolster the longer-run supply side of the U.S. economy. The bulk of the measures was contained in the 2001 Economic Growth and Tax Relief Reconciliation Act (EGTRRA), which introduced phased reductions in personal income tax rates and the gradual elimination of the estate tax. Relatively minor additional tax cuts were introduced in 2002, but in 2003, legislation was enacted that accelerated the previ-

---

[1]The U.S. fiscal year runs from October through September.

[2]The calculation of cyclical factors has been complicated by the sharp increase in capital gains tax revenues during the stock market boom of the 1990s. The CBO does not treat these revenues as a cyclical factor, but they clearly need to be excluded for identifying policy-related factors. Hence, Figure 1.2 includes a cyclically adjusted balance that has been corrected for the deviation of capital gains tax revenues from their historical average.

[3]Some studies have suggested a lesser contribution from cyclical factors, partly reflecting difficulties in distinguishing cyclical

effects from structural shifts in the economy. For example, Leidy (1998) found that only about 20–25 percent of the fiscal improvement between FY1992 and FY1997 was caused by the cycle. He estimated that roughly half the turnaround was accounted for by tax measures and another one-fourth by reductions in discretionary spending relative to GDP.

[4]Both the Office of Management and Budget and the CBO regularly present a decomposition of changes in the budget balance into cyclical and other factors.

[5]Discretionary spending is controlled by annual appropriations acts. Mandatory spending is provided by permanent law and does not require annual appropriations to ensure the continuation of spending.

Table 1.1. Factors Explaining the Budget Turnaround
(Data relate to unified budget balance including the Social Security surplus)

	Billions of U.S. dollars			Percent of Total Change		
	FY2002	FY2003	FY2004–08 (cumulative)	FY2002	FY2003	FY2004–08 (cumulative)
Office of Management and Budget (OMB)						
Budget balance						
April 2001 current services baseline	283	334	2,578	…	…	…
FY2004 *Mid-Session Review* projection	–158	–455	–1,455	…	…	…
Change in budget balance	–441	–789	–4,034	100	100	100
Of which						
Economic and technical reestimates	–284	–418	–1,782	64	53	44
War, homeland, and other enacted legislation	–63	–193	–723	14	24	18
Tax relief	–93	–177	–1,022	21	22	25
2001 EGTRRA	–41	–94	–761	9	12	19
2002 JCWAA	–52	–38	19	12	5	0
2003 JGTRRA	…	–45	–280	…	6	7
Pending budget proposals	…	–1	–506	…	0	13
Congressional Budget Office (CBO)						
Budget balance						
January 2001 current services baseline	313	359	2,543	…	…	…
CBO baseline projection, August 2003	–158	–401	–1,446	…	…	…
Change in budget balance	–471	–760	–3,989	100	100	100
Of which						
Economic and technical reestimates	–306	–427	–1,871	65	56	47
War, homeland, and other enacted legislation	–55	–138	–1,185	18	18	30
Tax relief	–9	–195	–933	17	26	23
2001 EGTRRA	0	–93	–677	8	12	17
2002 JCWAA	–1	–40	17	9	5	0
2003 JGTRRA	…	–62	–273	…	8	7

Sources: OMB, *Mid-Session Review, Budget of the U.S. Government, FY2004* (July 2003); CBO, various publications; and IMF staff calculations.
Note: EGTRRA = Economic Growth and Tax Relief Reconciliation Act; JCWAA = Job Creation and Worker Assistance Act; JGTRRA = Jobs and Growth Tax Relief Reconciliation Act.

ously scheduled tax cuts and also added additional elements, including a significant reduction in the tax rate applying to dividends and capital gains (Box 1.1).

The major tax cuts (as well as some spending measures) enacted in 2001 and 2003 have been estimated to have cost roughly $1.7 trillion over FY2002–FY2011. However, substantial debate and uncertainty have surrounded these cost estimates, largely reflecting the complicated and nontransparent manner in which the measures have been enacted. For example, some measures are only effective for a short period, while others—such as the elimination of the estate tax—are being phased in so that the fiscal cost will rise in the coming years. Moreover, all tax measures are subject to sunset clauses, which will mean that rates and deductions will—in the absence of policy action—return to pre-2001 levels in 2011 at the latest. However, it is the administration's stated intention to make the tax cuts permanent, which would leave the federal budget deficit roughly 2 percent of GDP above its baseline level by FY2013.

Figure 1.3. Federal Expenditures
(In percent of GDP)

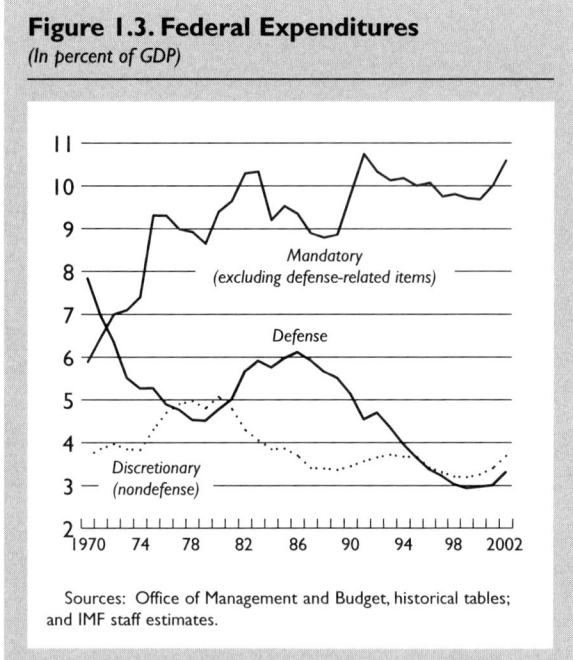

Sources: Office of Management and Budget, historical tables; and IMF staff estimates.

Costs and Consequences of Tax Cuts and Deficits

The sharp erosion in the fiscal position and the recent emphasis on tax cuts have revived a long-standing debate about the extent to which fiscal deficits crowd out private investment, and whether tax cuts, by improving economic incentives, can significantly boost the economy's supply side.

The current administration has played an active role in this debate.[6] It has emphasized that tax cuts would carry important longer-run supply-side benefits that could help mitigate their budgetary cost. The administration has also stressed that the federal deficit and debt-to-GDP ratios that are projected over the coming 5–10 years are "manageable" and remain well below the peak levels recorded in the 1980s and early 1990s.

There is little doubt that significant macroeconomic gains could be reaped from reforms of the U.S. tax code, with the Council of Economic Advisers (CEA, 2003) citing estimates of potential gains in the range of 2–6 percent of GDP. The tax system places a disproportionate burden on personal and corporate incomes, compared with a consumption-based tax system, discourages labor market participation and saving, and is, hence, economically less efficient. The administration's 2003 proposals were

viewed as a significant move toward a consumption-based tax system, because the initial package of measures announced in February would have lowered marginal income tax rates, eliminated the double taxation of dividends, and significantly expanded the extent to which income earned on saving would have been tax free.

Moreover, tax reform that simplified the system could also yield significant gains, given that the multitude of tax deductions and exemptions have imposed considerable administrative and other costs. As noted in CEA (2003), taxpayers are required to spend roughly 3 billion hours a year dealing with federal tax matters, and overall compliance costs are estimated at around 10 percent of total federal tax revenues.

It remains an open question whether the tax cuts adopted since early 2001 will have significant supply-side benefits:

- Although the cuts in income tax rates will—at the margin—improve incentives to work, the labor participation rate is already high, and empirical studies do not suggest that it is highly tax elastic (Angrist, 1991; Blundell, Duncan, and Meghir, 1998).[7]

- Moreover, in their final form, the tax measures appear to have taken only modest steps toward shifting the tax burden from income to consumption. Although tax rates on dividends and capital gains were lowered, the administration was not successful in eliminating the double taxation of corporate income or expanding the deductibility of saving from income. Moreover, there is considerable academic debate about the likely magnitude of any supply-side benefits from reducing taxes on dividends. For example, it has recently been argued that the effect on capital spending would be minimal, especially because increased dividend payouts could reduce funds available for new capital spending (e.g., Gale and Orszag, 2003).

- The measures also did little to address the complexity of the U.S. tax system. A number of the originally proposed simplifications did not pass, including on tax-preferred savings instruments. Indeed, in many respects the legislation appeared to have only added to the complexity of the system, for example, by using phase-ins

---

[6]See, for example, the discussion in OMB (2003a).

[7]At the same time, the short-term demand effect of the tax cuts is likely to have been limited by the fact that higher-income households tend to derive most of the income gains from tax reform (Gruber and Saez, 2000) but generally have a lower marginal propensity to consume than lower-income households (e.g., Gross and Souleles, 2001).

and sunsets to obscure the true budget cost and expanding the number of tax preferences.

The modest efficiency gains that might arise from the recent tax cuts will also have to be weighed against the effects of a prolonged period of fiscal weakness. As shown in Figure 1.4, the FY2004 budget is expected to result in deficits well into the next decade—a substantial deterioration compared with the January 2002 current services baseline, which saw a return to budgetary surpluses around 2007.

Although the deficit ratio is expected to narrow somewhat as the economy recovers in coming years, there are important reasons to worry that these projections may still prove optimistic (Figure 1.5). The strict limits on discretionary spending that have been assumed may be difficult to sustain, especially because of pressures to increase outlays on defense and homeland security, as yet undefined supporting policies for ensuring that limits on other discretionary programs are adhered to, and reduced pressure to maintain spending discipline as a result of the expiration of the Budget Enforcement Act (BEA).[8] Also, there are significant uncertainties about tax revenue projections. Notably, the official budget projections do not take into account the costs of reforming the Alternative Minimum Tax (AMT), and are predicated on the assumption that the recent (and still not fully understood) sharp drop in personal tax revenue will be largely reversed.[9]

With U.S. fiscal deficits expected to persist into the foreseeable future, will any supply-side benefits be outweighed by the effect of weaker public saving on interest rates and investment? The Council of Economic Advisers (2003) argued strongly that these potential offsetting effects would be minimal. However, the estimates surveyed in Section II generally suggest that the short-term stimulus stemming from the FY2004 budget proposals is likely to wane in several years, with higher deficits beginning to crowd out private investment and dampen output thereafter. In one simulation, for example, the tax cuts would eventually lower U.S. productivity—in terms of labor output per hour—by ½ percent in the long run.

Global Issues

Although U.S. fiscal policy has undoubtedly provided valuable support to the global economy in recent years, large U.S. fiscal deficits also pose significant risks for the rest of the world. Simulations reported in Section II suggest that a 15 percentage point increase in the U.S. public debt ratio projected over the next decade would eventually raise real interest rates in industrial countries by an average of ½–1 percentage point. Higher borrowing costs abroad would mean that the adverse effects of U.S. fiscal deficits would spill over into global investment and output.

Moreover, against the background of a record-high U.S. current account deficit and a ballooning U.S. net foreign liability position, the emergence of twin fiscal and current account deficits has given rise to renewed concern. The United States is on course to increase its net external liabilities to around 40 percent of GDP within the next few years—an unprecedented level of external debt for a large industrial country (IMF, 2003b). This trend is likely to continue to put pressure on the U.S. dollar, particularly because the current account deficit increasingly reflects low saving rather than high investment.

Although the dollar's adjustment could occur gradually over an extended period, the possible global risks of a disorderly exchange rate adjustment, especially to financial markets, cannot be ignored. Episodes of rapid dollar adjustments failed to inflict significant damage in the past, but with U.S. net external debt at record levels, an abrupt weakening of investor sentiments vis-à-vis the dollar could possibly lead to adverse consequences both domestically and abroad.[10]

Long-Run Insolvency of Social Security and Medicare

From a long-term perspective, higher U.S. fiscal deficits are especially worrisome because of the precarious financial position of the Social Security and Medicare systems. Although U.S. demographics compare relatively favorably with most other industrialized nations (see discussion in Section III), both systems are projected to run sizable deficits about a

---

[8]For example, the administration's $87 billion supplemental to cover the costs of ongoing military operations and reconstruction in Afghanistan and Iraq was about twice the size expected at the time the staff projections underlying Figure 1.5 were made.

[9]The AMT is a parallel income tax system with fewer exemptions, deductions, and rates than the regular income tax (e.g., personal exemptions and the standard deduction are not allowed under the AMT). It was enacted to limit the extent to which high-income taxpayers can reduce their tax liability by using preferences in the regular tax code. Due to increases in nominal income, the number of tax returns subject to the AMT is projected to increase from 4 million in 2004 to 33 million in 2010.

[10]In a March 2003 speech, delivered at a Bank of France symposium, Federal Reserve Chairman Alan Greenspan remarked on the U.S. current account deficit: "There are limits to the accumulation of net claims against an economy that persistent current account deficits imply. The cost of servicing such claims adds to the current account deficit and, under certain circumstances, can be destabilizing."

Box 1.1. Recent U.S. Tax Initiatives

Economic Growth and Tax Relief Reconciliation Act (EGTRRA) of 2001

Significant tax cuts were legislated as part of the EGTRRA in April 2001. The measures included

- a phased reduction in the individual income tax rate over the period 2001–06, with the top rate falling from 39.6 to 35 percent and the 28, 31, and 36 percent rates falling by 3 percentage points; and the creation of a 10 percent bracket for lower incomes, with an increase in the income threshold applicable to this bracket scheduled for 2008;

- a gradual elimination of the estate tax by 2010, with increases in exemptions and reductions in rates during 2002–09 and repeal of the tax in 2010;

- phased increases in the child tax credit from $500 in 2001 to $1,000 in 2010;

- marriage penalty relief, in the form of a phased increase in the standard deduction for married couples filing jointly to twice that for single taxpayers during 2005–09, and a phased increase in the income threshold for the 15 percent rate bracket during 2005–08;

- alternative minimum tax (AMT) relief through an increase in exemptions by $2,000 for single taxpayers and $4,000 for joint taxpayers during 2001–04.

The 10-year cost of the measures was held to $1.35 trillion by phasing them in gradually and allowing them to expire after 2010 (that is, all tax rates were to revert to their 2001 level by the end of 2010).

Job Creation and Worker Assistance Act (JCWAA) of 2002

Additional tax initiatives were included in the economic stimulus package signed into law in March 2002. The package was estimated to cost $97 billion over FY2002–FY2003 and included

- an allowance for businesses to take an additional first-year depreciation deduction of 30 percent on certain investments made during the three years after September 10, 2001;

- temporal extension of the business loss-carry forward rule from two to five years;

- tax cuts for New York City businesses damaged by the September 11 terrorist attacks.

Jobs and Growth Tax Relief Reconciliation Act (JGTRRA) of 2003

Further tax cuts were proposed in February 2003 as a part of the administration's FY2004 budget. The measures were estimated to cost a cumulative $1.3 trillion over FY2004–13, and included

- an economic growth package that would bring forward to 2003 the previously scheduled reductions in marginal tax rates, increases in the child tax credit, and marriage penalty relief; eliminate the double taxation of dividends; and provide temporary tax incentives for businesses investment (at a cost of $726 billion over 10 years);

- other tax incentives, including measures to encourage saving, charitable giving, and health care; unemployment insurance reform; and tax simplification (at a cost of $114 billion);

- permanent extension of expiring tax provisions, including the 2001 cuts (at a cost of $588 billion).

The economic growth package was passed in the form of JGTRRA in May 2003, while other budget proposals were not legislated as of September 2003. However, JGTTRA contained only parts of the administration's growth package. Dividends were not fully excluded from personal income tax, and some

---

decade from now when the baby boom generation enters its peak retirement years, and accumulated surpluses are exhausted 10–20 years thereafter.

The Social Security system is under pressure as a result of both the declining fertility rate—which (unlike in many other countries) is somewhat offset by higher immigration—and increases in longevity. As a result, the dependency ratio—the ratio of retirees to the working-age population—is projected to rise from 20 percent at present to around 40 percent by the middle of the century. This implies that payroll tax revenues will decline while social security spending is expected to roughly double as a proportion of GDP (Figure 1.6). The financial position of the Medicare and Medicaid systems is considerably worse, given the rapid growth of health care costs and the modest share of benefits that is covered by individual contributions. Medicare expenditures are projected to grow almost threefold relative to GDP over the next five decades, and considerable increases are also likely in the case of Medicaid.[11]

The projected sharp increase in expenditures, relative to contributions, and the rapid increase in health care costs mean that the Social Security and Medicare systems are highly underfunded. Unless steps are taken to adjust contribution rates and benefits, the programs will fall into deficit in the next two

---

[11]Cost increases for Medicaid are less strongly driven by demographic developments, since benefits are provided to all low-income households independent of age.

measures were made subject to sunsets in order to contain the total cost to $350 billion through FY2013. The package consisted of the following:

- the tax rate on capital gains was lowered to 15 percent from 20 percent and was also applied to dividends. The 10 percent rate applied to capital gains of low-income households was to be reduced in phases to zero percent by 2008. These measures would expire after 2008;

- the tax rate reductions scheduled for 2004 and 2006 were brought forward to 2003. However, the rates would still revert to pre-2001 levels after 2010. The expansion of the 10 percent income bracket scheduled for 2008 was brought forward to 2003 but is set to expire after 2007;

- marriage penalty relief was brought forward to 2003 but set to expire after 2004;

- the child tax credit was increased from $600 to $1,000 in 2003 and 2004, reverting to $500 in 2011;

- AMT exemption levels were increased in 2003–05 by $4,000 for single taxpayers and $8,000 for married taxpayers filing joint returns, reverting to previous levels thereafter;

- the annual deduction for small business investment was increased to $100,000 with expanded eligibility, and the first-year depreciation for some capital expenses was raised to 50 percent, with both measures expiring after 2004.

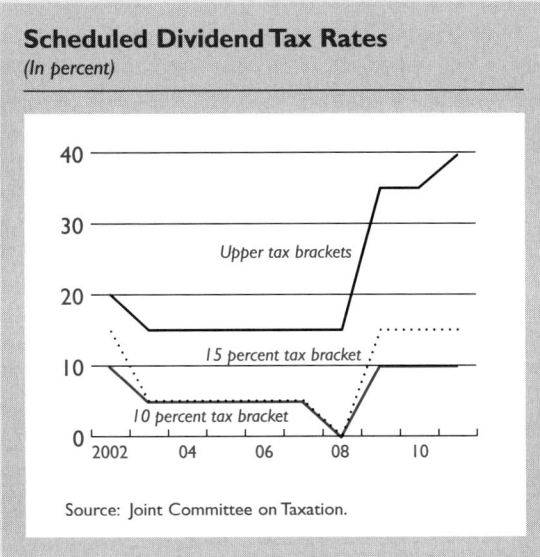

Scheduled Dividend Tax Rates
(In percent)

Upper tax brackets

15 percent tax bracket

10 percent tax bracket

Source: Joint Committee on Taxation.

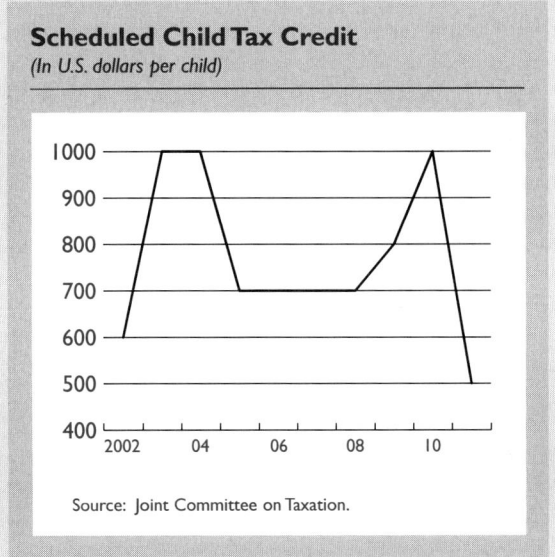

Scheduled Child Tax Credit
(In U.S. dollars per child)

Source: Joint Committee on Taxation.

decades and have to be supported by growing transfers out of the federal general fund. IMF staff simulations of the rapid increase of federal debt that would result—which are similar to those presented by the CBO and the administration's FY2004 budget—are shown in Figure 1.7.

Official estimates place the net present value of the programs' unfunded actuarial liability at around 160 percent of current GDP, if measured over a 75-year horizon.[12] But even these estimates understate the financial problems facing these programs because, in the absence of policy action, the pro-

grams will be running large cash flow deficits past this projection horizon. Moreover, closing the fiscal gap can be accomplished through a variety of policy measures (e.g., tax hikes, spending cuts, and so on) and at varying speed, both of which have different implications that are not captured by typical actuarial measures.

These considerations have led to a renewed emphasis on estimates of the fiscal gap, which take into account longer horizons and the intergenerational transfers that are involved. Section IV presents estimates of the U.S. fiscal imbalance using an intergenerational accounting framework that encompasses the entire federal fiscal system over an infinite horizon. The results suggest that the fiscal imbalance is as high as $47 trillion, nearly 500 percent of cur-

---

[12]OMB, 2003a, Chapter 3. This estimate assumes that current assets of the Social Security Trust Fund will be used to cover future pension benefits.

rent GDP, and that closing this fiscal gap would require an immediate and permanent 60 percent hike in the federal income tax yield, or a 50 percent cut in Social Security and Medicare benefits. The analysis also illustrates that this gap is associated with a severe intergenerational imbalance, with the burden on future generations increasing further if corrective measures are delayed.

The Policy Challenge

To restore a sustainable position, U.S. fiscal policy must refocus on two key objectives. The first is to adopt a clear and credible policy framework to achieve a balanced budget (excluding the Social Security surplus) over the cycle. The second is to pursue the reforms needed to place the Social Security and Medicare systems on a sound financial footing.

Restoring Budget Balance

Balancing the budget, excluding Social Security, has been an underlying goal of U.S. fiscal policy since at least 1985, when this objective was enshrined in the Gramm-Rudman-Hollings legislation. It is also an objective that the current administration has endorsed in the past—for example, the FY2002 budget was committed to saving the entire Social Security surplus, allowing almost all out-standing federal debt to be repaid over 10 years. The focus on balanced budgets is grounded in the realization that today's Social Security surpluses represent an accumulation of contributions by program participants that need to be saved to fund future retirement benefits.

With the approaching retirement of the baby boom generation, reestablishing a balanced U.S. federal deficit is becoming increasingly urgent. Achieving this objective over a 5–10-year period would leave the government debt ratio more than 10 percent of GDP lower in 2013 than at present and provide much-needed room for designing and implementing the reform of entitlement programs in advance of the demographic shock (see Figure 1.7 for an illustration). Returning to a balanced budget would also help ensure that the eventual adjustment of the U.S. current account deficit is orderly and rests on stronger national saving rather than weaker U.S. investment and growth.[13]

How large a fiscal adjustment would be needed to meet this objective? The CBO's August 2003 baseline suggests that the effort would need to be significant. For example, assuming that the recent tax cuts are made permanent, amendments to the Medicare system are implemented, and steps are taken to

---

[13]Federal Reserve Chairman Greenspan also made this point in his February 2002 speech to the National Summit on Retirement Savings.

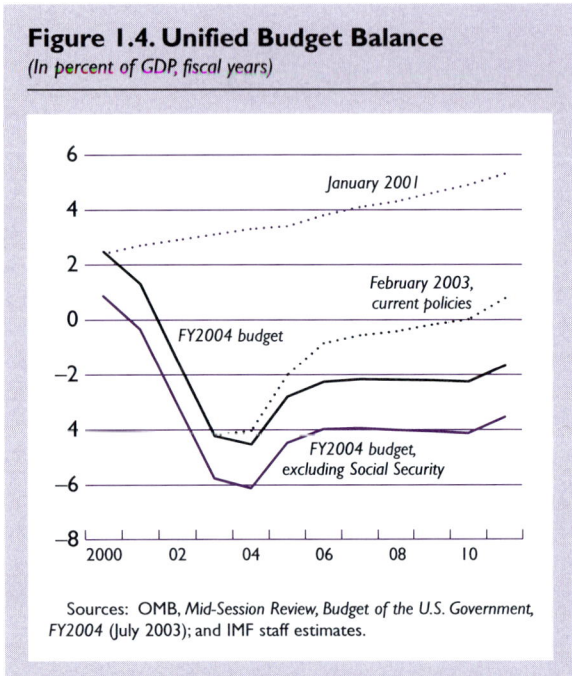

Figure 1.4. Unified Budget Balance
(In percent of GDP, fiscal years)

Sources: OMB, *Mid-Session Review, Budget of the U.S. Government, FY2004* (July 2003); and IMF staff estimates.

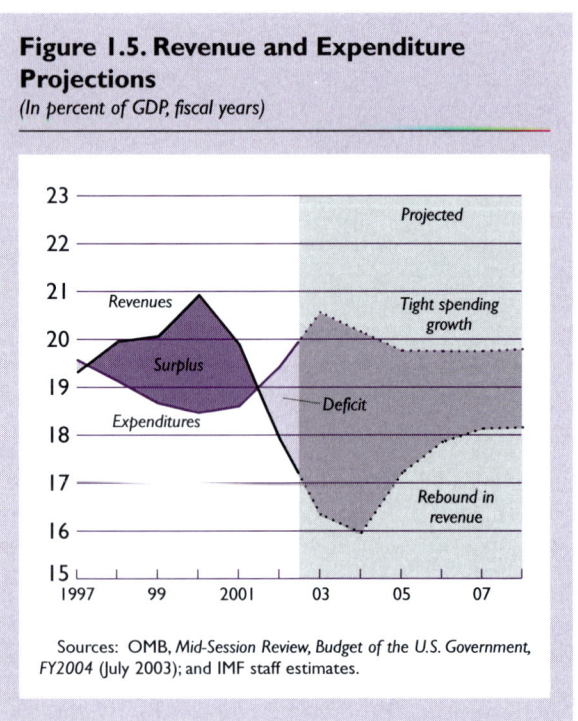

Figure 1.5. Revenue and Expenditure Projections
(In percent of GDP, fiscal years)

Sources: OMB, *Mid-Session Review, Budget of the U.S. Government, FY2004* (July 2003); and IMF staff estimates.

address the reform of the Alternative Minimum Tax system, the unified budget deficit would fall to around 1½ percent of GDP in 2013. This measure still includes the surplus of the Social Security Trust Fund, however, which is classified as an "off-budget" item in the U.S. fiscal accounts. Once this surplus is excluded, the budget deficit, and the measures needed for balance, would be over 3 percent of GDP.[14] However, these estimates assume that extremely strict limits on discretionary spending—which keeps spending constant in real terms—are maintained for 10 years, and even larger shortfalls can be envisaged.

Given the magnitude of this adjustment, it would seem likely that both revenue measures and sustained spending restraints would need to be considered. On the revenue side, allowing the tax cuts to expire would yield around 2 percent of GDP, including the associated interest saving, but any revenue effort would also need to look for opportunities to expand the tax base. Recent CBO publications have illustrated that substantial revenues could be derived from reducing corporate and personal income tax preferences—including corporate tax shelters and mortgage interest deductibility. Section V suggests that energy taxes, which are comparatively light in the United States, could help meet the administra-

tion's environmental objectives while also providing substantial support for fiscal consolidation.

These measures would have to go hand-in-hand with a tightening of expenditure discipline, which weakened significantly with the emergence of surpluses in the late 1990s. In recent years, geopolitical considerations and the war on terrorism have compounded spending pressures, but these and other spending priorities will need to be weighed carefully if the adjustment burden is not to fall more heavily on the revenue side.

To support efforts to rein in public spending, greater weight could be given to reintroducing and strengthening the budget rules contained in the Budget Enforcement Act (BEA), which expired in October 2002. The international and U.S. experience is that fiscal adjustment tends to be more effective if it is based on formal rules embedded in a fiscal policy framework with clearly defined medium- and long-term objectives, similar to the fiscal responsibility legislation adopted by a number of industrial countries. Such a framework—and the political consensus that would surround it—could help provide policymakers with an appropriate basis for facing the difficult trade-offs in the period ahead.

A similar conclusion has been reached by a recent IMF report on U.S. fiscal transparency, which generally praised the high degree of transparency in the United States but noted a lack of clarity in the longer-term direction of its fiscal policy (Box 1.2). Fiscal responsibility legislation could also help guard against using accounting devices that obscure

---

[14]The Social Security surplus reflects an accumulation of assets that is—in principle—matched by future obligations to retirees. For this reason, U.S. policymakers and other analysts have often focused on measures of the fiscal balance that exclude the Social Security surplus.

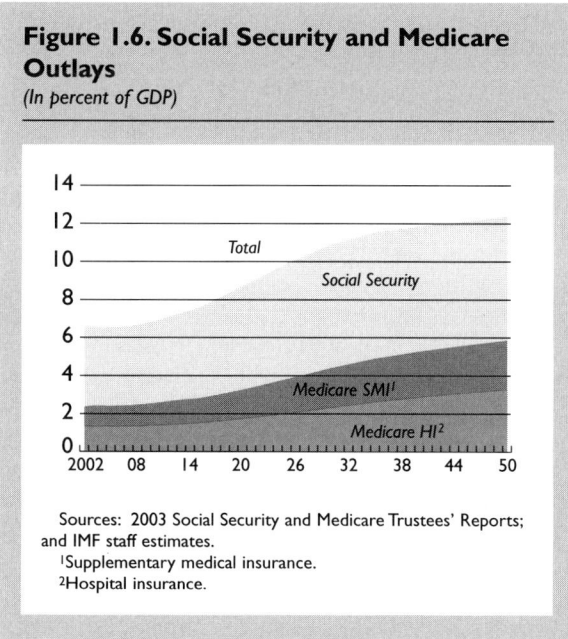

Figure 1.6. Social Security and Medicare Outlays
(In percent of GDP)

Sources: 2003 Social Security and Medicare Trustees' Reports; and IMF staff estimates.
[1]Supplementary medical insurance.
[2]Hospital insurance.

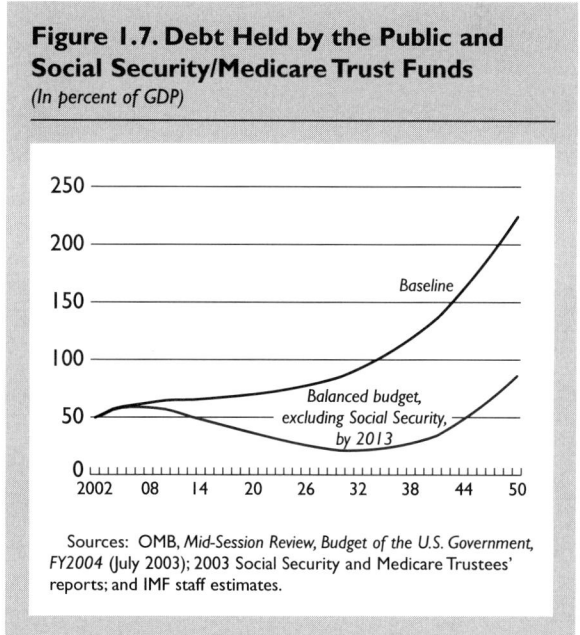

Figure 1.7. Debt Held by the Public and Social Security/Medicare Trust Funds
(In percent of GDP)

Sources: OMB, *Mid-Session Review, Budget of the U.S. Government, FY2004* (July 2003); 2003 Social Security and Medicare Trustees' reports; and IMF staff estimates.

Box 1.2. Fiscal Transparency in the United States

During November 2002–February 2003, a staff team conducted a review of fiscal transparency in the United States in relation to the IMF's Code of Good Practices on Fiscal Transparency (IMF, 2003a). The principal conclusions of that review are as follows:

- The United States is fully compliant with most elements of the Fund's Code of Good Practices on Fiscal Transparency and sets best practice standards in many areas. The U.S. Constitution provides a strong and well-tested framework that clearly defines the roles of the executive and legislative branches in fiscal management. The Congress plays a central role in shaping the budget, which ensures a highly open process. State and local governments also have clearly defined fiscal responsibilities, operating independently from the federal government, and are subject to market discipline. Budget documentation is easily accessible to the public, timely, comprehensive, and reliable, and it excels in its scope and quality of analysis.

- Nevertheless, there remains a lack of clarity about the longer-term direction of fiscal policy. This partly reflects the sheer size of the federal government and the complexity of the congressional budget process. Major efforts have been made over the past three decades to put in place a legal framework to strengthen this aspect of the budget process. However, with the expiration of the Budget Enforcement Act (BEA), the failure of Congress to pass a budget resolution for FY2003, and the recent uncertainty regarding the permanence of tax cuts and the costs of the war in Iraq, budget decisions do not seem presently guided by clear medium- and long-term fiscal policy objectives.

- Budget responsibility legislation to replace the BEA could help provide a basis for a more systematic incorporation of longer-term considerations into the budget process. Building on existing budget requirements and practices, such a budget framework could require the specification and justification of medium-term fiscal targets as part of the President's budget; a budget report on long-term fiscal policy; discretionary spending caps and pay-as-you-go (PAYGO) requirements for mandatory spending and revenue; and clearer procedures for specifying and disclosing key budget assumptions (e.g., with respect to expiring legislation).

- Fiscal transparency could be strengthened in a number of additional ways: reporting an internationally comparable measure of the budget balance to supplement the unified budget presentation; providing an overview of state and local government finances as part of the federal budget presentation; annually assessing the costs and risks associated with the quasi-fiscal activities; including a comprehensive statement on fiscal risks in budget documents; reconsidering the legal basis for tax expenditure reporting; ensuring that audit reports of agencies by the General Accounting Office (GAO) are followed up, possibly by a standing public accounts committee that reports to Congress; increasing the emphasis on program performance; and paying greater attention to the full cost of providing government services.

---

the true cost of measures and lead to loss of credibility, as appears to have been the case in recent years. Section VI shows that the caps on discretionary outlays and pay-as-you-go (PAYGO) requirements contained in the BEA strongly contributed to the successful fiscal consolidation in the United States during the 1990s. Although the BEA's constraints were increasingly circumvented just prior to its expiration, Section VI suggests a range of options for further strengthening these types of budget rules.

Reforming Entitlement Programs

Although the impact of population aging will not be felt fully until well into the next decade, and public debt ratios are not expected to rise before 2020, the long lead times required in reforming pension and health insurance programs suggest that policy actions need to be taken well in advance. For example, the 1983 reform of the Social Security system raised the normal retirement age from 65 to 67, but to allow workers to adjust their saving and retirement plans, the increase was scheduled to be phased in over a 25-year period, beginning only in 2002.

At this stage, relatively modest changes would still appear to be sufficient to close projected pension shortfalls. For example, an immediate 2 percentage point hike in the Social Security payroll tax could be sufficient to close the system's 75-year actuarial liability. However, payroll taxes in the United States are already high and further increases would tend to be regressive and could adversely affect incentives to hire labor. Other options include measures to stem the growth of benefits, including by indexing the calculation of pension benefits to the consumer price index (CPI) rather than wages, further increasing the normal retirement age, or reducing the benefits for early retirement. In general, however, the longer such decisions are delayed, the larger and more painful the required adjustments will be.

Privatizing Social Security could, in principle, provide a framework for addressing the system's unfunded liability, but would still require either cuts in benefits or hikes in premiums, as well as an explicit recognition of the liabilities that the system has already accrued. Moreover, the higher returns that might be earned from personal retirement accounts would have to be weighed against the increased exposure of retirement savings to market fluctuations, which would likely require the government to still provide a minimum safety net for retirees. Questions have also been raised about the administrative costs that would have to be borne in managing small accounts, and the challenge of designing a system that discourages workers from withdrawing excessive amounts at retirement and imposing a burden on the rest of the system.

Medicare reform is even more critical. The Medicare trust fund begins to run into deficit in 2016, and the unfunded actuarial liability (in net present value terms) has been estimated at 130 percent of current GDP. This raises the question of whether it would have been prudent to defer an extension of benefits, including to cover prescription drugs, until credible measures to address the system's longer-term financial problems are established. Indeed, the broader weakness of the U.S. health care system—which has left health care spending the highest among OECD countries (relative to GDP), without a commensurately high ranking in public health indicators (see Figure 1.8)—suggests that more sweeping reforms of the system may be needed.

State and Federal Fiscal Relations

A review of the U.S. fiscal situation would be incomplete without considering the relatively sharp deterioration of state and local government finances in recent years. In aggregate, this sector accounts for close to half of general government spending, raising concern that expenditure cutbacks on the state and local levels could offset some of the stimulus provided by the federal government. This issue is addressed in Section VII, which reviews the principal causes of the state and local fiscal crisis and attempts to quantify its macroeconomic implications. Rising deficits have been caused both by shrinking corporate and personal income tax revenues and by sharp increases in cyclical and health-related spending—in part reflecting tax cuts and more generous benefit levels granted during the boom years of the 1990s. With budget reserves being increasingly eroded, further adjustment measures will be needed. However, the aggregate size of local and state government cutbacks is estimated to be only a small fraction of the overall stimulus provided

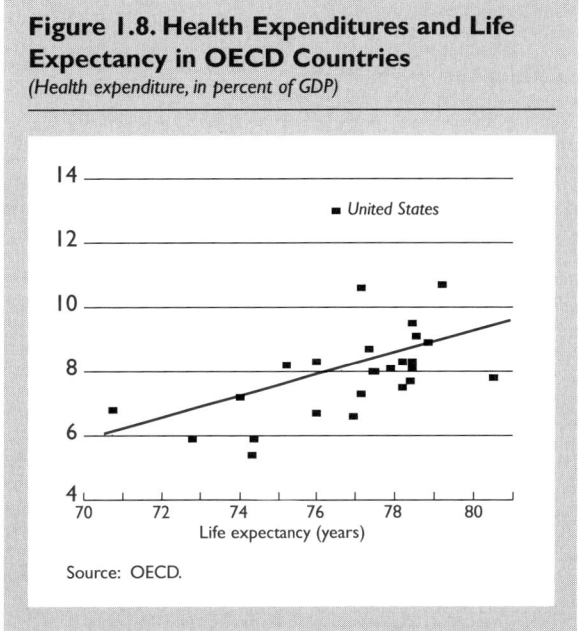

Figure 1.8. Health Expenditures and Life Expectancy in OECD Countries
(Health expenditure, in percent of GDP)

Source: OECD.

by the federal government, and their macroeconomic impact is likely to remain small.

Concluding Remarks

Meaningful reforms of entitlement programs such as Social Security and Medicare tend to require long lead times, given their impact on intergenerational income distribution and politically controversial nature. To reach broad-based agreement on such reforms, fiscal resources are often required to smooth the transition and ensure that reform measures can be implemented over a politically acceptable time horizon. Only a few years ago, the conditions for movement on these fronts seemed to be in place in the United States, with the demographic shock still half a generation away and government debt set to be all but eliminated within a decade. Since then, however, a combination of cyclical, geopolitical, and policy factors have erased a decade's worth of fiscal consolidation, just a short time before the retirement of the baby boom generation begins.

The discussion in this and subsequent sections suggests that the U.S. fiscal problem is still manageable, and there remains a window of opportunity for reform. However, the experience of recent decades has shown that fiscal consolidation is difficult to achieve and perhaps even more difficult to hold on to. Therefore, the room for maneuver is narrowing quickly.

References

Angrist, J., 1991, "Grouped-Data Estimation and Testing in Simple Labor-Supply Models," *Journal of Econometrics*, Vol. 47, No. 2/3, pp. 243–66.

Blundell, R., A. Duncan, and C. Meghir, 1998, "Estimating Labor Supply Responses Using Tax Reforms," *Econometrica*, Vol. 66, No. 4, pp. 827–62.

Congressional Budget Office (CBO), 2003, *The Budget and Economic Outlook: Fiscal Years 2004–2013* (Washington: U.S. Government Printing Office).

Council of Economic Advisers (CEA), 2003, *Economic Report of the President, February 2003* (Washington: U.S. Government Printing Office).

Gale, W.G., and P.R. Orszag, 2003, "The Administration's Proposal to Cut Dividend and Capital Gains Taxes," Tax Notes (Washington: Urban Institute, Brookings Institution), January. Available via Internet: www.taxpolicycenter.org/commentary/taxnotes.cfm.

Gross, D.B., and N.S. Souleles, 2001, "Do Liquidity Constraints and Interest Rates Matter for Consumer Behavior? Evidence from Credit Card Data," NBER Working Paper No. 8314 (Cambridge, Massachusetts: National Bureau of Economic Research).

Gruber, J., and E. Saez, 2000, "The Elasticity of Taxable Income: Evidence and Implications," NBER Working Paper No. 7512 (Cambridge, Massachusetts: National Bureau of Economic Research).

International Monetary Fund, 2003a, *United States: Report on the Observance of Standards and Codes—Fiscal Transparency Module*, IMF Staff Country Report No. 03/243 (Washington: International Monetary Fund).

———, 2003b, *World Economic Outlook, September 2003: Public Debt in Emerging Markets* (Washington: International Monetary Fund).

Leidy, M., 1998, "A Postmortem on the Achievement of Federal Fiscal Balance," in *United States: Selected Issues*, IMF Staff Country Report No. 98/105 (Washington: International Monetary Fund).

Office of Management and Budget (OMB), 2003a, *Budget of the U.S. Government, Fiscal Year 2004* (Washington: U.S. Government Printing Office).

———, 2003b, *Mid-Session Review, Budget of the U.S. Government, FY2004* (Washington: U.S. Government Printing Office), July.

II   Economic Impact of U.S. Budget Policies

Roberto Cardarelli and Ayhan Kose

The U.S. fiscal position has deteriorated significantly in recent years. In 2000, the Congressional Budget Office (CBO) projected surpluses in the range of 3 percent of GDP for the next 10 years and for the federal debt to be nearly paid down by 2010. Since then, partly because of the economic downturn, but also reflecting policy initiatives to boost spending and cut taxes, the budgetary balance has swung into substantial deficit. The fiscal deficit seems likely to reach over 4 percent of GDP in FY2004 and to remain significant well into the future.

The turnaround in the fiscal situation—and calls for further tax cuts—have revived the long-standing debate about the macroeconomic impact of fiscal policies. On the one side has been the view that tax cuts generate positive supply-side benefits sufficient to offset the negative effects of higher fiscal deficits on interest rates and lower private investment (CEA, 2003a). Others, however, have questioned the size of the supply-side benefits, and have argued that higher deficits would ultimately lower output.

This discussion tends to support the view that budget deficits have adverse effects in the longer run, both domestically and abroad. In particular, model-based simulations on the administration's FY2004 budget proposals, as well as a review of the recent crowding-out literature, suggest that recent U.S. fiscal policies would boost output in the short run, but, in the longer run, larger deficits would tend to cause interest rates to rise above and output to fall below baseline.[1] Moreover, empirical evidence suggests that higher levels of U.S. public debt would have undesirable spillovers, causing an increase in global interest rates.

Simulations of the FY2004 Budget Proposal

Previous episodes of large fiscal expansion in the United States raise questions about the effectiveness of fiscal stimulus. There are three recent cases in which the federal fiscal balance fell by at least 1½ percent of GDP, in cyclically adjusted terms, over a two-year period (Figure 2.1). In the first episode, during 1965–67, structural outlays rose by 1¾ percent of GDP, mainly because of military spending on the Vietnam war. In the second and third episodes, tax cuts caused structural revenues to fall by 1 percent of GDP during 1974 and 1976 and by 2¼ percent of GDP during 1981–83, respectively. Although the tax cuts were associated with some acceleration in real GDP growth over subsequent three-year periods, real GDP growth declined, or remained essentially unchanged, in each of the subsequent 10 years (Table 2.1).

Simulations of the FY2004 budget proposals also suggest that the short-term stimulus would wane quickly. Table 2.2 summarizes the results of analyses of the FY2004 budget proposals, mainly based on U.S. macroeconometric models maintained by Macroeconomic Advisers (MA) and Global Insight

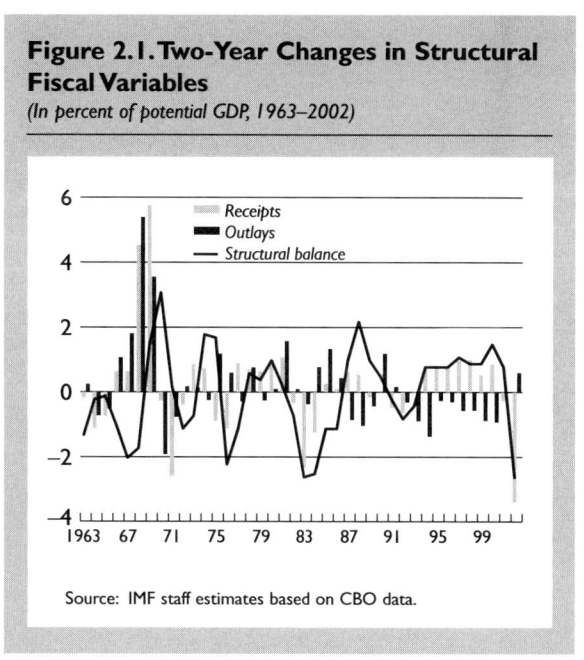

Figure 2.1. Two-Year Changes in Structural Fiscal Variables
(In percent of potential GDP, 1963–2002)

Source: IMF staff estimates based on CBO data.

---

[1]See Section I for a description of the administration's original FY2004 budget proposals and of the tax legislation that was passed in May 2003.

Table 2.1. Change in Real GDP Growth Before and After Large Fiscal Expansions
(In percent)

	1965–67	1974–76	1981–83
Post–3-year average less pre–3-year average	–2.1	1.7	3.3
Post–10-year average less pre–10-year average	–1.1	–0.3	0.3

Source: IMF staff estimates.

(GI). Both models predict that the proposals would have a significant positive effect on output growth over the next two years. However, the boost to aggregate demand would be more modest thereafter because of the crowding out of private investment from higher real interest rates.[2]

Most analyses indicate that the budget would dampen output in the long term. In most macroeconomic models, the decline in public and national saving implied by the FY2004 budget proposals would lead to higher real interest rates and lower capital

accumulation—for example, in the MA model the effect is to lower labor productivity by about ½ percentage point in 2017, relative to the baseline scenario (Figure 2.2).

This result is confirmed by a CBO (2003) study that examines the budget proposals from the perspective of several alternative models. In a "textbook" neoclassical growth model, in which economic agents do not modify their behavior in response to expected future policy changes, the budget would lower GDP by ¾ percent below the baseline during 2009–13. Using life-cycle and infinite-horizon models, in which economic agents are forward looking, the CBO shows that the budget proposals would only increase long-run output if the tax cuts were anticipated to be reversed in the future. In this case, households work and save more to be able to pay for future taxes, offsetting the crowding-

[2]The studies differ somewhat from each other. The CBO study examines the implications of the entire FY2004 budget proposals, whereas the others focus only on the Economic Growth Package. The study does not report which model is used but notes that "the particular values of the numerical estimates presented reflect judgments regarding the implementation of the proposals" (CEA, 2003b, p. 8).

Table 2.2. Estimates from Large-Scale Models
(Real GDP growth, change from baseline; in percent)

Study by: Model Used:	CEA[1] n.a.	CBO[2] MA	CBO[2] GI	MA[3] MA	GI[4] GI	HF[5] GI	Average
2003	0.4	0.5	0.4	0.5	0.2	0.3	0.4
2004	1.1	1.3	1.3	1.0	0.8	0.6	1.0
2003–07 (average)	0.2	0.6	1.3	0.0	0.1	0.1	0.4

[1]Council of Economic Advisers (2003b).
[2]Congressional Budget Office (2003).
[3]Macroeconomic Advisers (2003).
[4]Global Insight (see Newport, 2003).
[5]Heritage Foundation (see Beach and others, 2003).

out effect (Table 2.3).[3] The CBO's analysis also illustrates that, in an open economy context, net inflows of foreign capital can help offset the decline in national saving and alleviate crowding out.

Fiscal Deficits and Real Interest Rates

A key indicator of the extent to which budget policies risk crowding out private investment is their impact on interest rates. Consequently, most empirical analysis of crowding out has focused on the relationship between fiscal deficits and interest rates. This literature is summarized below.

Simulations of large-scale macroeconometric models generally indicate that budget deficits have a sizable effect on interest rates. In these models, the size of crowding out typically depends on the monetary policy reaction function, the interest rate sensitivity of investment, the openness of the economy, and on how expectations of future policies are modeled.[4] In a recent survey, Gale and Orszag (2002)

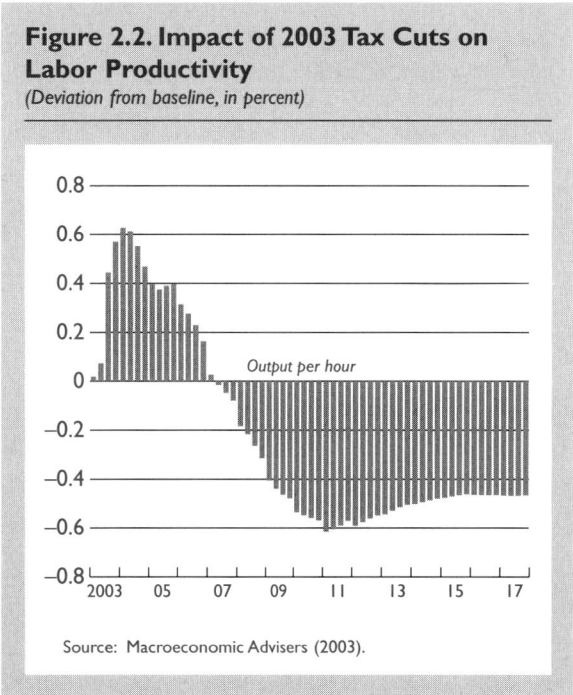

Figure 2.2. Impact of 2003 Tax Cuts on Labor Productivity
(Deviation from baseline, in percent)

Output per hour

Source: Macroeconomic Advisers (2003).

[3]In the "textbook" growth model, labor supply increases because of lower marginal tax rates, but output declines because higher government and private consumption crowd out capital accumulation. It is only when expectations of higher taxes after 2013 induce additional savings that the tax cuts have a positive impact on savings, investment, and output (as in the two models with forward-looking agents). This effect is larger in an infinite-horizon model because agents take into account the higher tax burden on their descendants. In all models, maximum effect is achieved if the future increase in taxation is sought through higher lump-sum taxes. Estimates assuming an increase in future marginal tax rates fall in the range of those presented in Table 2.3.

[4]For a brief description of some of these models in the context of a dynamic scoring analysis of fiscal policy measures, including

found that the average prediction of this type of models is that a 1 percentage point increase in the primary deficit-to-GDP ratio, caused by a tax cut, is followed by a 40 basis point increase in long-term interest rates after one year, and a 60 basis point increase after 10 years. This compares to an increase of 60 basis points and 130 basis points, respectively,

two large-scale structural models of the U.S. economy used by the Federal Reserve, see Mauskopf and Reifschneider (1997).

Table 2.3. Estimates from Small-Scale Models
(Average change in GDP from CBO's baseline, in percent)

	2004–08	2009–13
Textbook growth model	–0.2	–0.7
Closed economy life-cycle growth model		
Lower government consumption after 2013	–0.3	–1.5
Higher lump-sum taxes after 2013	0.5	0.3
Open economy life-cycle growth model		
Lower government consumption after 2013	–0.6	–0.5
Higher lump-sum taxes after 2013	0.3	0.6
Infinite horizon growth model		
Lower government consumption after 2013	0.2	–0.6
Higher lump-sum taxes after 2013	0.9	1.4

Source: CBO (2003).

if the same increase in the primary deficit is induced by higher government spending.

Econometric estimates of reduced-form models have often provided conflicting results on the relationship between fiscal deficits and interest rates. This likely reflects the difficulty that studies have faced in taking into account the extent to which long-term interest rates respond to expectations of future fiscal policies, rather than to the current policy stance.[5] More recent papers that address this issue have found a positive and significant impact of expected budget deficits on expected future interest rates—averaging 35 basis points for a 1 percentage point increase in the deficit-to-GDP ratio, roughly in line with the estimates of the large-scale models (see Table 2.4).[6]

The administration's FY2004 budget proposals were accompanied by estimates of much smaller effects of deficits on interest rates. These estimates were based on a neoclassical framework developed by Elmendorf and Mankiw (1999), in which real interest rates in the steady state equal the marginal productivity of capital, which in turn depends on the capital share of income and the income-to-capital ratio. Using historical averages for these parameters, and assuming that a one-dollar increase in public debt reduces the long-run stock of capital by 60 cents, a 1 percentage point increase in the debt-to-GDP ratio leads to an increase of real interest rates of only around 2–3 basis points (CEA, 2003a).[7]

However, these arguments do not provide significant comfort. For example, Laubach (2003) notes that the estimates above would be consistent with an increase of interest rates of approximately 15 basis points following a permanent 1 percentage point increase in the deficit-to-GDP ratio. Moreover, while the CEA's analysis suggests a relatively modest interest rate effect, this is predicated on a substantial degree of crowding out. In the CEA's example, a 5 percent of GDP increase in government debt would lower the capital stock by around 3 percent of GDP, which, given estimates of the gross marginal productivity of capital of around 10 percent, would be consistent with a permanent reduction in output of roughly one-third of a percent.

[5]Among the studies that find no statistically significant relationship between fiscal deficits and interest rate are the ones by Plosser (1987) and Evans (1987), which proxied expected fiscal deficits using forecasts from vector autoregressive models (VAR). However, the usefulness of this method to capture actual expectations is subject to a series of limitations (Elmendorf, 1993).

[6]A caveat for these results is that the reduced-form relationship between expectations of future budget deficits and interest rates could be driven by changes in the expectations of output growth. However, Elmendorf (1996) shows that this relationship is robust to the explicit introduction of a variable capturing expectations on the future state of the business cycle.

[7]The assumption made by CEA (2003a) is that, while private savings do not respond at all to the increase in public debt, around a third of the decrease in national savings is offset by larger capital flows from abroad.

Table 2.4. Selected Studies on the Impact of Deficits on Real Interest Rates

	Crowding-Out Effect (in basis points)[1]	Interest Rates Considered	Fiscal Variable	Business Cycle Regressor
Laubach (2003)	23	10-year Treasury bond yield expected over the next 5 years	CBO 5-year-ahead forecast	No
Laubach (2003)	36	5-year Treasury bond yield expected over the next 5 years	OMB 5-year-ahead forecast	No
Laubach (2003)	9	10-year Treasury bond yield	CBO 5-year-ahead forecast	No
Canzoneri, Cumba, and Diba (2002)	60	Slope of yield curve (10-year note less 3-month bill)	CBO 5-year-ahead forecast	No
Canzoneri, Cumba, and Diba (2002)	40	Slope of yield curve (10-year note less 3-month bill)	CBO 10-year-ahead forecast	No
Elmendorf (1993)	49	Change in 3-year Treasury bond yield	DRI forecast of deficit-to-GDP ratio	Unemployment rate

[1]Increase in interest rates caused by a 1 percentage point rise in the deficit-to-GDP ratio.

Table 2.5. Correlations of G-7 Real Interest Rates (1977–2002)[1]

	Canada	Germany	United Kingdom	Japan	United States	France	Italy
Canada	1						
Germany	0.7	1					
United Kingdom	0.6	0.4	1				
Japan	0.7	0.7	0.5	1			
United States	0.6	0.3	0.5	0.5	1		
France	0.6	0.5	0.6	0.7	0.5	1	
Italy	0.7	0.5	0.7	0.5	0.5	0.8	1
World	0.8	0.8	0.7	0.8	0.6	0.8	0.8

Source: OECD.

[1]Interest rates are 12-month Euromarket interest rates deflated by the same period CPI inflation rate. The world real interest rate is the simple average of national rates.

International Implications of Higher U.S. Public Debt

The integration of capital markets over the last three decades suggests the possibility of important spillovers from U.S. fiscal policy to the rest of the world. Higher fiscal deficits and public debt in one country will tend to absorb global savings and might cause higher world interest rates. This proposition is examined below.

Country-specific real interest rates have tended to move together over the last three decades. Table 2.5 shows that the real interest rate correlations for industrialized countries are all positive and generally quite high, which, some authors have argued, suggests the existence of a "world" real interest rate.[8] Figure 2.3 shows the evolution of different proxies for this rate: the unweighted average of the national rates, their GDP-weighted average, and a measure based on the first principal component of the national rates. Each of these indices significantly increased during most of the 1980s, a period of rapid growth of world public debt, but declined over most of the next decade despite still-high levels of world public debt.

Several studies have suggested that "world" fiscal policy matters for determining national real interest rates. Net public debt is found to be a significant

determinant of the "world" real interest rate in Helbling and Wescott (1995) and of national real interest rates in Orr and Conway (2002). Ford and Laxton (1999) estimate the impact of world government net debt and consumption on national real interest rates

Figure 2.3. World Government Net Debt-to-GDP Ratio and World Real Interest Rate
(In percent)

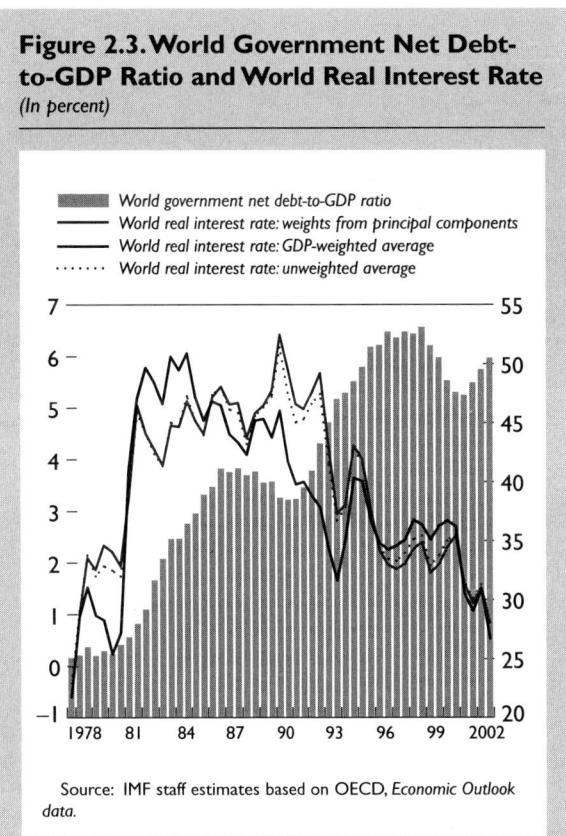

Source: IMF staff estimates based on OECD, *Economic Outlook* data.

---

[8]Using panel data techniques, Gagnon and Unferth (1995) show that national real interest rates do not persistently deviate from a common world interest rate, defined as the simple average of the rates of nine OECD countries. The only exception seems to be the United States, a result that the authors suggest may reflect the country's lower trade integration with the rest of the world. On the correlations reported in Table 2.5, note that since 1999 the European countries that joined the euro have essentially shared the same interest rate.

of selected industrialized countries. They find that a 1 percentage point increase in world net government debt raises real interest rates by around 20 basis points. The main results and estimation methodologies adopted by these three papers are reported in Table 2.6.

We reexamined the relationship between national real interest rates and world public debt. The sample comprises 11 industrial countries—the G-7 countries plus Belgium, Denmark, the Netherlands, and Switzerland—over the period 1977–2002. The interest rates used are the 12-month Euromarket interest rates on certificates of deposits, deflated by the same-period CPI inflation rate. We used two approaches: first, each country's real interest rate

was regressed by ordinary least squares (OLS) on two world fiscal variables, namely the net public debt-to-GDP ratio and the share of real GDP absorbed by government consumption and investment.[9] Second, the data were pooled and the 11

---

[9]This captures the two channels through which fiscal policy is supposed to crowd out private investments: the "portfolio" channel (via higher public debt) and the "transaction" channel (via higher government spending). Following Ford and Laxton (1999), the change in real government consumption is also used as a regressor. As economic theory suggests that both the fiscal variables, expressed as a share of GDP, and the real interest rates are stationary, no attempt is made to estimate a long-run relationship between these variables using a cointegration approach.

Table 2.6. Selected Studies on the Impact of World Fiscal Variables on Real Interest Rates[1]

Authors	Crowding-Out Effect (in basis points)[1]	Interest Rates Considered as Dependent Variable	Fiscal Regressor	Expected Inflation	Methodology and Period
Helbling and Wescott (1995)	16–20	World (GDP-weighted) 3-month Treasury bill yield.	World (GDP-weighted) gross government debt-to-GDP ratio.	Exponential smoothing.	Cointegration analysis through dynamic OLS and error correction model (1960–93).
Helbling and Wescott (1995)	37–50	World (GDP-weighted) 3-month Treasury bill yield.	World (GDP-weighted) net government debt-to-GDP ratio.	Exponential smoothing.	Cointegration analysis through dynamic OLS and error correction model (1960–93).
Helbling and Wescott (1995)	0–13	World (GDP-weighted) 10-year Treasury bond yield.	World (GDP-weighted) gross government debt-to-GDP ratio.	Exponential smoothing.	Cointegration analysis through dynamic OLS and error correction model (1960–93).
Helbling and Wescott (1995)	16–42	World (GDP-weighted) 10-year Treasury bond yield.	World (GDP-weighted) net government debt-to-GDP ratio.	Exponential smoothing.	Cointegration analysis through dynamic OLS and error correction model (1960–93).
Ford and Laxton (1999)	17–23	National 12-month Euromarket certificates of deposits' interest rate.	World (GDP-weighted) net government debt-to-GDP ratio.	Same year CPI inflation rate.	Pooled OLS and SURE time series estimation, imposing equality of coefficients across countries (1977–97).
Orr and Conway (2002)	16	National 10-year government bond yields.	National net government debt-to-GDP ratio.	Hodrick-Prescott filter of CPI inflation rate.	Error correction model estimation, imposing equality of long-term coefficients across countries (1986:1–2002:1, countries: Australia, Canada, Germany, New Zealand, Sweden, United Kingdom, United States).

[1]Increase in interest rates caused by a 1 percentage point increase in the government debt-to-GDP ratio.

Table 2.7. OLS Regressions of Real Interest Rates on World Fiscal Variables[1]

	c	WGND[2]	WGA[3]	DWGA[4]	R^2	DW	Wu-Hausman Test[5] WGND	WGA
Belgium	−16.31 (0.20)	−0.05 (0.34)	1.07 (0.04)	1.13 (0.38)	0.50	0.59	−2.49	−0.52
Canada	−29.48 (0.02)	0.11 (0.04)	1.36 (0.01)	−2.08 (0.16)	0.17	0.65	−2.92	−1.03
Switzerland	−12.95 (0.23)	0.08 (0.11)	0.54 (0.20)	−0.05 (0.95)	0.10	1.00	−1.98	−0.13
Germany	−9.38 (0.36)	0.01 (0.82)	0.57 (0.15)	1.52 (0.24)	0.16	0.61	−2.85	0.65
Denmark	−48.70 (0.00)	0.10 (0.02)	2.29 (0.00)	1.29 (0.20)	0.48	0.59	−1.41	0.14
United Kingdom	−53.50 (0.00)	0.26 (0.00)	2.18 (0.00)	−1.14 (0.36)	0.38	0.67	−3.26	0.74
Japan	−40.05 (0.00)	0.07 (0.29)	1.86 (0.00)	1.16 (0.35)	0.49	0.46	−3.86	1.05
Netherlands	−26.31 (0.04)	0.00 (0.91)	1.38 (0.01)	−0.31 (0.86)	0.34	0.44	−3.01	0.33
United States	−25.20 (0.30)	0.06 (0.55)	1.21 (0.21)	−2.32 (0.20)	0.14	0.31	−1.05	−0.63
France	−67.10 (0.00)	0.23 (0.00)	2.89 (0.00)	0.48 (0.55)	0.42	0.63	−1.52	−0.26
Italy	−71.95 (0.00)	0.27 (0.00)	3.02 (0.00)	−1.69 (0.27)	0.45	0.89	−1.62	−0.99

Source: Authors' calculations.

[1]Data are semiannual from 1977:1 to 2002:2; p-values from Newey-West heteroskedasticity and autocorrelation-consistent standard errors are reported in parentheses. The dependent variables are the national 12-month Euromarket interest rates deflated by the same period CPI inflation rate.

[2]WGND is the GDP-weighted average of national net government debt-to-GDP ratio, with the only exclusion of Switzerland. GDP is converted using purchasing power parity exchange rates.

[3]WGA is the GDP-weighted average of national real government absorption (consumption plus investment) as a share of GDP.

[4]DWGA is the first difference of WGA.

[5]t-statistics of the Wu-Hausman test for the exogeneity of WGND and WGA. The null hypothesis is exogeneity. The list of instruments used comprises the second and third lags of WGND and WGA. Critical values are from the standardized normal distribution (10 percent = ±1.28, and 5 percent = ±1.64).

equations were estimated as a system, imposing the constraint that the coefficients of the fiscal variables were the same across all countries.[10] Instrumental variables were used to avoid potential biases stemming from the dependence of public debt on interest rates.[11] The system estimates were derived using a generalized method of moment (GMM) estimation methodology, which yields consistent

---

[10]This approach improves the efficiency of the estimators if disturbances are correlated across countries and also increases significantly the degrees of freedom because it allows estimating the coefficients of the fiscal variables using a much larger number of observations.

[11]The list of instruments consists of the lagged values of the world net government debt-to-GDP ratio plus the other fiscal regressors, which are taken as predetermined. The Wu-Hausman test reported in Table 2.7 supports this choice, because it failed to exclude the exogeneity of the world net public debt-to-GDP ratio in the interest rates OLS regressions, while it could not rule out the exogeneity of government consumption. This may reflect that government consumption does not include interest paid on the stock of debt.

and asymptotically normal estimators under relatively unrestrictive assumptions on the error term and regressors.

The regression results generally confirm that an increase in world public debt affects national real interest rates but cannot rule out the existence of a break in the relationship over the 1990s. The OLS coefficients of the world fiscal variables have the right signs, but only in a few cases are significant at a 5 percent level (Table 2.7). The results also indicate that augmenting the OLS regressions with the country-specific public debt-to-GDP ratios does little to improve the results, as this coefficient is rarely both significant and positive.

The system estimates show that both world public debt and government absorption are significant determinants of national real interest rates. A 1 percentage point increase in the world government debt-to-GDP ratio induces an increase in national real interest rates of around 10 basis points over the 1997–2002 period (Table 2.8). This result is robust to the addition of other variables, such as those capturing the business cycle and monetary policy and inflation changes, although the relatively scarce number

Table 2.8. Joint GMM Estimation of National Real Interest Rates Imposing Equality of Coefficients Across Equations[1]

WNGD[2]	0.12 (0.00)	0.09 (0.00)	0.15 (0.00)	0.15 (0.00)	0.16 (0.00)	0.13 (0.00)
WGA[2]	1.34 (0.00)	1.34 (0.00)	1.67 (0.00)	1.66 (0.00)	1.92 (0.00)	2.79 (0.00)
DWGA[2]	1.24 (0.00)	−0.04 (0.88)	1.10 (0.00)	0.86 (0.00)	0.62 (0.05)	1.41 (0.00)
Euro dummy[3]	−1.47 (0.00)	−0.68 (0.01)	−0.94 (0.00)	−0.88 (0.00)	−0.75 (0.00)	−0.32 (0.02)
UNE[4]		0.47 (0.00)				
DINFL[5]			0.20 (0.00)			
DIRS[6]				0.14 (0.00)		
LAF[7]					0.17 (0.27)	
PBAL[8]						0.99 (0.00)
J-statistic[9]	2.75 (0.99)	10.80 (0.46)	0.11 (0.99)	0.11 (0.99)	7.23 (0.78)	5.58 (0.89)

[1]Data are semiannual from 1977:1 to 2002:2. Total system observations: 566. p-values are in parentheses. The heteroskedasticity and autocorrelation-consistent covariance matrix is estimated based on the Newey and West estimator. The vector of instruments comprises the second and third lags of WNGD and the other regressors.

[2]See Table 2.7.

[3]Dummy for 1999:1–2002:2.

[4]World (GDP-weighted) unemployment rate.

[5]Change in world (GDP-weighted) CPI inflation rate.

[6]Change in world (GDP-weighted) short-term real interest rate (CPI inflation deflated).

[7]World (GDP-weighted) labor force growth.

[8]Change in world (GDP-weighted) primary balance.

[9]Model specification test. The null is that the model is well specified. Critical values are from a chi-square distribution with 11 degrees of freedom (equal to the number of overidentifying restrictions in the system).

of available observations makes it difficult to test for the stability of the coefficients over the period considered.[12] Moreover, as most of the desirable properties of GMM estimators are only valid asymptotically, the point estimates should be taken with caution.

With these caveats in mind, the estimates suggest that the 15 percentage point increase in the U.S. public debt ratio, projected by the CBO to result from recent budget measures, would lead to an average ½–1 percentage point increase in national real interest rates over the next decade.

References

Beach, W.W., R.A. Rector, A. Goyburu, and N.J. Michel, 2003, "The Economic and Fiscal Effects of the President's Growth Package," Center for Data Analysis Report No. 03–05 (Washington: Heritage Foundation), April 16.

Canzoneri, M., R. Cumby, and B. Diba, 2002, "Should Central Bank and the Federal Reserve Be Concerned About Fiscal Policy?" in *Rethinking Stabilization Policy* (Kansas City: Federal Reserve Bank of Kansas City).

Congressional Budget Office (CBO), 2003, *An Analysis of the President's Budgetary Proposals for Fiscal Year 2004* (Washington: U.S. Government Printing Office).

Council of Economic Advisers (CEA), 2003a, *Economic Report of the President* (Washington: U.S. Government Printing Office).

———, 2003b, "Strengthening America's Economy: The President's Jobs and Growth Proposals" (Washington: U.S. Government Printing Office).

Elmendorf, D.W., 1993, "Actual Budget Deficit Expectations and Interest Rates," Harvard Institute of Economic Research Discussion Paper No. 1639 (Cambridge, Massachusetts: Harvard University).

———, 1996, "The Effect of Deficit-Reduction Laws on Real Interest Rates," Federal Reserve Board Finance and Economics Discussion Paper Series No. 1996/44 (Washington: Federal Reserve Board).

———, and N.G. Mankiw, 1999, "Government Debt," in *Handbook of Macroeconomics*, Vol. 1c, edited by J.B. Taylor and M. Woodford (Amsterdam: Elsevier).

Evans, P., 1987, "Do Budget Deficits Raise Nominal Interest Rates? Evidence from Six Countries," *Journal of Monetary Economics*, Vol. 20, No. 22, pp. 281–300.

Ford, R., and D. Laxton, 1999, "World Public Debt and Real Interest Rates," *Oxford Review of Economic Policy*, Vol. 15, No. 2, pp. 77–94.

Gagnon, J.E., and M.D. Unferth, 1995, "Is There a World Real Interest Rate?" *Journal of International Money and Finance*, Vol. 14, No. 6, pp. 845–55.

Gale, W., and P. Orszag, 2002, "The Economic Effects of Long-Term Fiscal Discipline," Urban-Brookings Tax Policy Center Discussion Paper No. 8 (Washington: Urban Institute, Brookings Institution), December 17. Available via Internet: www.taxpolicycenter.org/research.

Helbling, T., and R. Wescott, 1995, "The Global Real Interest Rate," in *Staff Studies for the World Economic Outlook* (Washington: International Monetary Fund).

Laubach, T., 2003, "New Evidence on the Interest Rate Effects of Budget Deficits and Debt," Federal Reserve Board Finance and Economics Discussion Paper Series No. 2003/12 (Washington: Federal Reserve Board).

Macroeconomic Advisers (MA), 2003, "A Preliminary Analysis of the President's Jobs and Growth Proposals" (unpublished; St. Louis, Missouri: Macroeconomic Advisers).

Mauskopf, E., and D.L. Reifschneider, 1997, "Dynamic Scoring, Fiscal Policy, and the Short-Run Behavior of the Macroeconomy," *National Tax Journal*, Vol. 50, No. 3, pp. 631–55. Available via Internet: ntj.tax.org.

Newport, P., 2003, "Bush Plan Boosts Short-Term U. S. Growth, but Adds to Deficits," *Global Insight*, February.

Orr, A., and P. Conway, 2002, "The GIRM: A Global Interest Rate Model," Westpac Institutional Bank Occasional Paper (Wellington, New Zealand: Westpac).

Plosser, C., 1987, "Fiscal Policy and the Term Structure," *Journal of Monetary Economics*, Vol. 20, No. 2, pp. 343–67.

[12]A Chow test on the stability of the coefficients in two subsamples of equal size rejects the null of stability.

III Social Security, Medicare, and U.S. Fiscal Prospects

Paula De Masi, Iryna Ivaschenko, and Christopher Towe

The reemergence of large U.S. budget deficits in recent years has heightened concern about the implications of demographic trends for the longer-term fiscal position.[1] In particular, with the tax cuts enacted in 2001 and 2003, and the higher levels of spending that have been introduced, substantial budget shortfalls are projected over the coming decade. With federal debt now rising as a share of GDP, the fiscal position seems to be considerably less well prepared to cope with the impending retirement of the baby boom generation, especially in view of the substantial actuarial deficits facing the Social Security and Medicare systems. In this section we describe the long-term fiscal challenges that result from these trends and briefly discuss recent Social Security and Medicare reform proposals.

Fiscal Consequences of Social Security and Medicare

Social Security and Medicare are the two principal federal programs in the United States that offer support for the elderly (Box 3.1). Social Security provides retirement income to the aged and is funded by the payroll taxes on the working age population. The Medicare system, which provides medical insurance for the elderly, is only partly funded by payroll taxes and retirees' premium payments, relying on transfers from the federal government for the balance of its resources.

Demographic and other pressures on these systems are expected to increase significantly in the coming decades. In particular, the retirement of the baby boom generation, a decline in the fertility rate, and an increase in longevity are projected to raise the dependency rate—the ratio of retirees to the working-age population—from around 20 percent at present to nearly 40 percent by the middle of the century. This will significantly increase the number of beneficiaries relative to the number of contributors in the Social Security system. Similar demo-

graphic pressures face the Medicare system, but in this case they are compounded by the rapid increases in medical care costs.

The trust funds for these systems currently run cash surpluses, but they are in significant deficit from an actuarial perspective. In FY2002, the combined Social Security and Medicare surplus was estimated at roughly 1 percent of GDP (excluding interest receipts), and the balances in their trust funds totaled over 15 percent of GDP. However, the programs are expected to run into deficit within the next two decades, which implies that the trust fund assets would eventually be exhausted. Indeed, over a 75-year projection period, Social Security and Medicare are estimated to have a combined unfunded liability—the shortfall between current assets and the net present value of projected inflows less projected payments to beneficiaries—at $16 trillion, or 160 percent of GDP:[2]

- The Old-Age, Survivors, and Disability Insurance (OASDI) system is projected to fall into deficit (excluding interest receipts) before 2020, with deficits rising to over 2 percent of GDP by the end of the 75-year projection horizon. The assets held by the OASDI trust funds are expected to be exhausted just after 2040, and the system has an unfunded liability estimated at around 35 percent of current GDP, equivalent to the revenue that would accrue to the system from an immediate and permanent increase in the payroll tax of 1.87 percentage points.

- The situation of the Medicare hospital insurance (HI) system is somewhat more difficult because its current surplus is more modest, the assets in its trust fund total only around 2 percent of GDP, and the rapid increase in health care costs is compounding the pressure of an increasing

---

[1]This section is a slightly revised and updated version of De Masi and Towe (2002).

[2]This estimate is contained in the administration's FY2004 budget. The subsequent discussion is based on IMF staff calculations, which in turn was based on the actuarial estimates contained in the Old Age, Survivors, and Disability Insurance (OASDI) and Medicare Trustees' reports (2003). Section IV contains an alternative calculation based on a generational accounting framework.

Box 3.1. Social Security and Medicare Systems

Social Security (OASDI)

- The Social Security system consists of the Old-Age and Survivors Insurance and the Disability Insurance systems. These two schemes are referred together under the acronym OASDI.

- Participation in the OASDI system is mandatory and near-universal. The programs are funded by a 12.4 percent payroll tax on labor income up to an inflation-adjusted ceiling—$87,000 in 2003. Although retirement benefits may be drawn as early as age 62, an unreduced pension is provided at the normal retirement age. The normal retirement age was 65 in 2002, but is scheduled, beginning in 2003, to increase gradually to 67 by 2027.

- Benefits are based on the average of monthly earnings of a worker's 35 highest-earning years prior to eligibility. In calculating postretirement benefits, preretirement earnings are indexed to average wage growth and postretirement benefits are indexed to CPI inflation. Monthly benefits are subject to a monthly maximum, which in 2003 was set at $1,404 for persons retiring at age 62, rising to $2,045 for persons retiring at age 70. Significant benefits are also paid in the event of death or disability prior to retirement.

- Both contributions and benefits are subject to tax. The employee's portion of the payroll tax—6.2 percentage points—is included in earned income for tax purposes. Benefits are included in taxable income according to a graduated formula—they are 100 percent excluded below a certain income threshold, with the exclusion rate falling to a minimum 15 percent at higher incomes. Taxes paid on up to 50 percent of benefits are returned to the OASDI system.

- The cash surpluses of the OASDI system are held in trust funds and invested in nonmarketable, interest-bearing government securities.

Medicare

- The Medicare program provides health insurance coverage for the elderly and disabled.

- Part A provides hospital insurance (HI) and is funded by a 2.9 percent payroll tax, which applies to income without a ceiling.

- Part B provides supplementary medical insurance (SMI) that covers the cost of physician and other services, and is funded in part by premiums paid by retirees. These cover only around 25 percent of SMI costs, with the balance coming from general government revenues.

- Typically, the Medicare system operates on a fee-for-service basis. Payment rates to providers are set by the Medicare system, and a deductible and copayment (typically 20 percent) by beneficiaries applies.

- The Medicare+Choice system was established to provide Medicare participants with the option of joining private managed care or fee-for-service plans. These privately run plans typically have lower copayment rates and allow a somewhat broader range of covered services but limit beneficiaries' access to prescribed providers. Enrollment in this program has been declining in recent years and it covers only around 10 percent of Medicare beneficiaries.

- The cash surpluses of the HI system are also held in a trust fund and invested in nonmarketable, interest-bearing government securities.

---

elderly population. The system is also projected to run annual deficits before 2020, which would grow to over 3½ percent of GDP by the end of the 75-year projection period. As a result, its unfunded liability is estimated at around 50 percent of GDP, equivalent to a 2.02 percentage point increase in the contribution rate.

- The position of the Medicare supplementary medical insurance (SMI) system is even more worrisome. The SMI system is run purely on a pay-as-you-go basis—that is, there are no trust fund assets that have been accrued—and premium payments cover only a part of its outlays. The administration's FY2003 budget estimated that the unfunded liability of the SMI system would be roughly an additional 80 percent of

GDP, equivalent to a 3.37 percentage point increase in the payroll tax.

Figure 3.1 illustrates the longer-term pressures on the system. For example, in the baseline scenario, both the OASDI and HI systems begin to run significant primary deficits in the next 20 years, with a substantial buildup of liabilities resulting soon thereafter. An immediate increase in payroll taxes to meet the actuarial deficit by the amounts described above would improve the situation but—despite tax rate increases that would total over 7 percentage points—the systems would still be left with substantial cash flow deficits in the longer run. By contrast, more modest cuts in benefit growth—for example, reducing the growth of OASDI benefits by ½ percentage point beginning in 2010 and slowing the pace of HI benefits by 1½ percentage points in the same year—would achieve actuarial balance and keep the cash flow deficits relatively modest over the 75-year projection period.[3]

The longer-run fiscal implications of these trends are significant. In the absence of reforms, outlays on Social Security and Medicare programs are projected to rise rapidly from around 7 percent of GDP at present to nearly 10 percent by 2023, increasing further to nearly 16 percent of GDP by the end of the 75-year horizon (Figure 3.2). Simple budget simulations show that, beginning in the next decade, these trends would cause the unified federal budget balance to erode sharply.[4] As a result, federal debt held by the public would increase rapidly after 2020 as spending pressures intensified.

The financial situation of the U.S. Social Security and Medicare systems is serious but still less dire than in many other industrial countries. In a recent OECD (2001) study, the United States was considered among the "slower-aging economies," compared with other industrial countries, because of its relatively high immigration and fertility rates, and relatively modest life expectancy. As a result, the projected increase in its age-related spending, including outlays for pensions and health care, was estimated to be at or somewhat less than average. In view of the U.S. system's relatively large trust fund assets and substantial contribution rate, its unfunded liability is also typically viewed as smaller than in other industrial countries. For example, Kohl and O'Brien (1998) estimate the unfunded liability of the Japanese, Italian, and Swedish systems as a share of GDP at 70 percent, 60 percent, and 132 percent, respectively.

President's Social Security Reform Commission

In early 2001, a presidential commission was established to examine options for reforming Social Security. Reform proposals were expected to adhere to several principles, which included (1) maintaining benefits for retirees and near-retirees, (2) avoiding any increase in social security taxes, (3) maintaining the survivor and disability benefits, (4) offering personal retirement accounts as a supplement to Social Security, and (5) avoiding investing Social Security trust funds in the stock market.

The Commission reported its findings in December 2001 (Social Security Commission, 2001) and suggested that reforms should include the following key elements:

- *Personal retirement accounts (PRAs).* Participants would be permitted to divert a portion—up to 4 percentage points—of their OASDI contributions to personal retirement accounts. OASDI benefits would be reduced by the amount of direct contributions to PRAs plus an implicit real return of up to 3½ percent.

- *Indexation.* The Commission suggested moving to a system in which the pensionable earnings of future retirees would be indexed to prices rather than wages, which, as illustrated above, would tend to lower the growth of benefits substantially. In addition, the formula for calculating benefits could be adjusted to increase its progressivity.

- *Minimum benefit.* In some of the reform options considered, a worker with 30 years of employment would be provided a minimum benefit of up to 120 percent of the poverty line.

Although the report argued that PRAs would have important advantages, including increasing the rate of return on employee contributions and possibly adding to national saving, it also illustrated that PRAs would exacerbate the system's insolvency. For example, diverting 2 percentage points from the OASDI payroll tax to fund PRAs would significantly reduce the cash flow available to meet current obligations. As a result, "transition payments" from general revenues to the trust funds would be needed over an extended period until benefit outlays were reduced to their new steady-state level. The net present value of these payments over the 75-year period would be equivalent to 10 percent of GDP.

The report also illustrated that reducing the generosity of the indexation of OASDI benefits would significantly improve the financial situation of the system, but that significant additional funding would still be required to close the system's actuarial deficit. For example, one reform option considered—which assumed amending the benefit formula, a relatively modest PRA, and the diversion of only 2½ percentage points of payroll taxes—would still require significant transition payments as well as a permanent increase in system financing equivalent to 0.63 percent of taxable payrolls.

---

[3]As detailed in the Trustees' reports, the projections are sensitive to underlying macroeconomic and demographic assumptions. Moreover, the projections assume that real interest rates remain significantly higher than the real growth rate of the economy, which significantly exacerbates the systems' debt dynamics.

[4]The simulations are based on the assumption that the balance for the non-Medicare, non-OASDI, and noninterest federal budget remains constant as a share of GDP after 2012; net interest payments on federal debt increase in line with the stock of debt; and OASDI and Medicare spending as a share of GDP rise in line with the projections made in the 2003 Trustees' reports.

Figure 3.1. Social Security and Medicare Projections
(In percent of GDP)

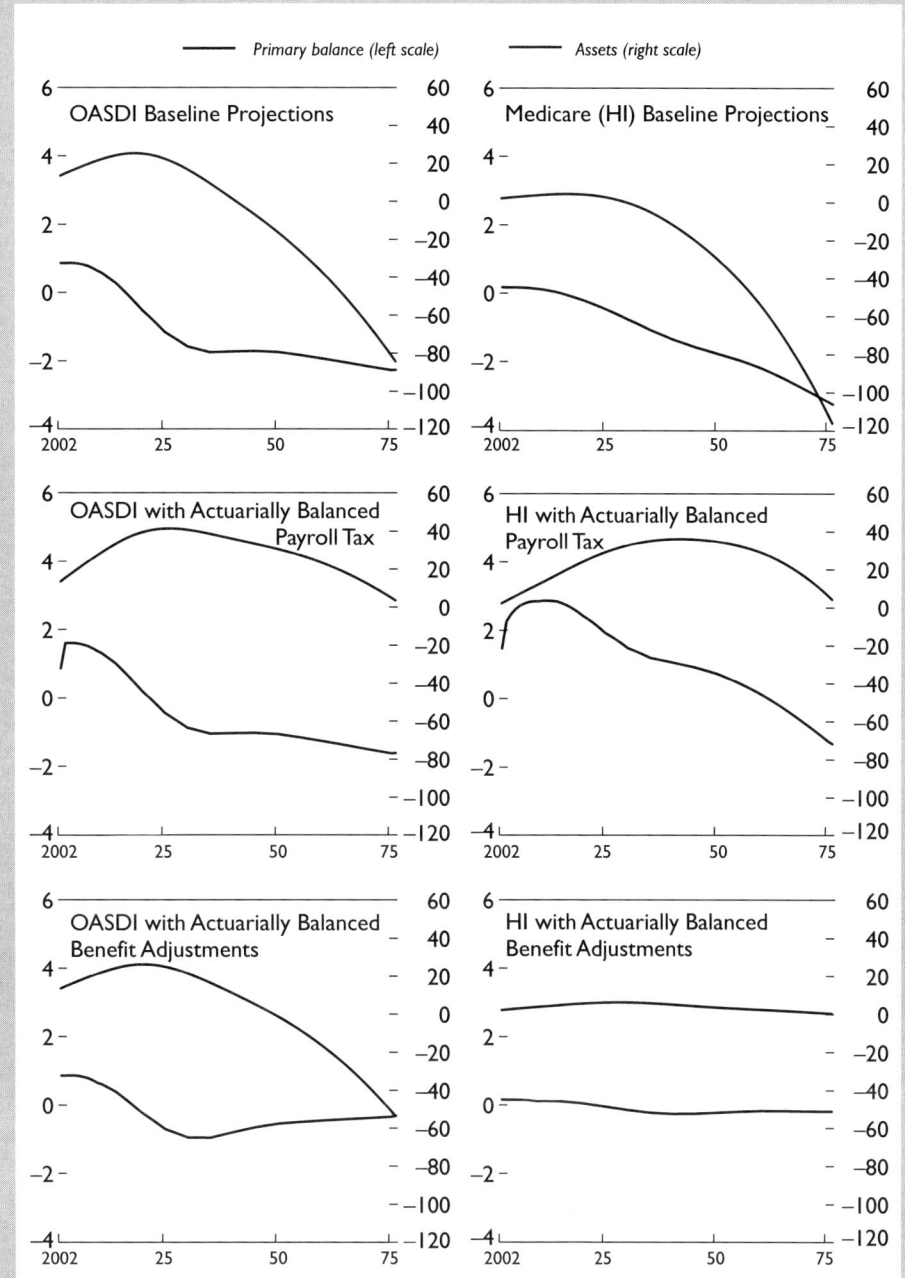

Source: Staff estimates based on long-range projections in the 2003 OASDI and Medicare Trustees' reports.
Note: OASDI = Old Age, Survivors, and Disability Insurance; HI = Hospital insurance. Benefit adjustments assume that, beginning in 2010, OASDI and HI benefits grow 0.5 percent and 1.6 percent slower than the baseline. The primary balance is equal to the difference between noninterest receipts and expenditure.

Figure 3.2. Budget Projections

(In percent of GDP)

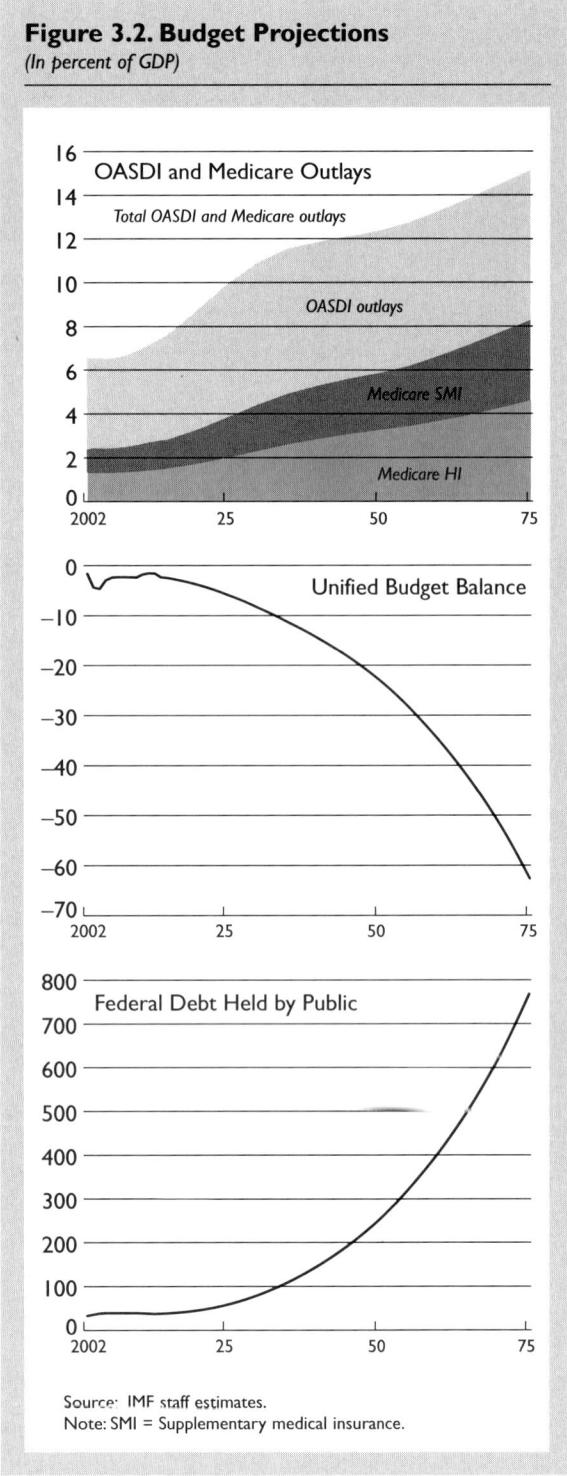

Source: IMF staff estimates.
Note: SMI = Supplementary medical insurance.

In addition to these considerations, significant technical and administrative issues would need to be resolved before such a system could be introduced:

- *Guarantees.* The Commission's reform proposals explicitly do not include a guaranteed minimum return on PRA investments. Since PRAs would be seen as a replacement of at least part of the existing OASDI entitlement, there may be pressure to attach at least some insurance to these accounts, which would increase their fiscal cost.

- *Tax issues.* The tax treatment of OASDI is somewhat anomalous because both contributions and benefits are taxable, and benefits are combined with other income in a formula that increases the progressivity of the system. It is unclear how PRAs would be treated, but to the extent that participants are able to voluntarily increase their contributions, there is a strong argument for affording these contributions a tax treatment similar to that of other retirement savings instruments, such as IRAs, 401(k)s, and so on.

- *Administrative issues.* The Commission appeared to favor PRAs held in the form of investment vehicles that would be somewhat constrained in both their portfolio allocation and payout schedule. This would minimize moral hazards related to excessive investment risk taking by participants and allow lump-sum distributions, as opposed to annuity payments, only to those retirees with demonstrably sufficient wealth. However, as a number of authors have noted, a system of annuities could be expensive to administer and would pose challenges for regulatory and tax policies.[5]

- *Benefits.* The report offers relatively limited options regarding cuts in OASDI benefits, and more stringent alternatives could be considered. For example, preretirement earnings and post-retirement benefits could be indexed to the CPI less an ad hoc adjustment for the bias it contains, or by the national accounts deflator for consumer expenditures. Consideration could also be given to increasing the pace at which the normal retirement age is increased or to lengthening the computation period for calculating benefits.

---

[5]The Congressional Budget Office (CBO, 2001b) notes, for example, that there would be a strong incentive for providers to discriminate among retirees according to risk class. Diamond and Orszag (2002) also note that the administrative costs of PRAs would likely be significantly larger in the initial years than assumed by the President's Commission, and these could be prohibitive when the size of accounts is small.

- *Supplemental security income (SSI).* The SSI system provides income support to low-income, elderly, and disabled persons, and is funded and administered separately from the OASDI system. The Commission's report acknowledges that reforms of the OASDI system should take into account the SSI system, and increases in the minimum OASDI benefits would likely need a corresponding increase in the SSI benefit.

There has been little progress toward implementing these or any other reforms since the Commission's report was issued, and the administration has simply called for further dialogue and debate on the way forward.

Medicare Reform

The last major revision of the Medicare system, which was included in the Balanced Budget Act of 1997, stemmed from a growing public awareness that the longer-term fiscal pressures facing the system were becoming more immediate. The 1997 legislation introduced a number of reforms that were mainly geared at containing costs.[6] For example, payments to physicians and hospitals were reduced, and to promote competition in health care delivery a wider variety of private plans, including health maintenance organizations (HMOs), provider-sponsored organizations, and preferred provider organizations, were permitted to contract with Medicare.

Since then, pressures have built to expand Medicare benefits, culminating in legislation in December 2003 that added a new prescription drug benefit. The benefit would involve copayments of 25 percent for initial annual payments up to $2,250, with a gap in coverage thereafter until out-of-pocket expenses reached $3,600, when copayments of only 5 percent would apply. Low-income retirees would be provided a more generous benefit, and significant subsidies would be directed to private plans to discourage employers from scaling back retiree benefits in response to the increase in Medicare coverage. The legislation also boosted Medicare premiums for high-income retirees and introduced, on a demonstration basis, a plan for private sector health plans to compete with the traditional Medicare system.

These proposals would significantly worsen Medicare's financial position, and estimates by the

Congressional Budget Office (CBO, 2003) suggest a total budgetary impact of $400 billion over 10 years, or $1/4$–$1/2$ percent of GDP annually by 2013. Moreover, concerns have been raised regarding the impact of the legislation on employers' willingness to retain retirees on existing plans, the absence of mechanisms for containing the growth of drug prices, and the risk that political pressures will cause a further enrichment of the benefit.

Recent studies have also raised significant doubts about the likely efficacy of private health care plans in controlling costs. For example, Gold and Achman (2003) examine the experience of participants in the "Medicare+Choice" system—an HMO-style system that has been running parallel to the traditional fee-for-service system since 1997. They find that out-of-pocket costs for enrollees have been significantly higher than in the traditional Medicare system. A study by the Medicare Payment Advisory Commission (2002) suggests that Medicare payment rates to health care providers are considerably lower than payment rates by private insurers—Medicare rates were found to be just under 80 percent of the private rate—reflecting the substantial market power that the Medicare system has been able to exert in setting rates.

CBO (2001a) laid out a comprehensive set of options for restoring the solvency of the Medicare system. These included increasing premium revenues; changing eligibility conditions to reduce the number of beneficiaries; reducing costs per beneficiary; and increasing payroll taxes. However, the question remains of whether even these measures would be sufficient in the absence of more fundamental reforms of the health care system, given the broader problem of a substantial uninsured population and a private health insurance system that has helped push overall health care spending in the United States to levels that exceed the OECD average by several percentage points of GDP.

Concluding Remarks

The Social Security and Medicare systems are likely to place significant longer-term pressures on the U.S. fiscal system, given demographic and other trends. Little progress has been made toward addressing the financial problems of the Medicare system, despite the very large deficits of the SMI and HI systems. The focus instead has been on expanding benefits in the area of prescription drugs rather than addressing the fundamental reforms that would assure the programs' longer-term solvency.

Specific proposals for reform of Social Security have recently been put forward by the President's Reform Commission. The Commission's report use-

---

[6]The Balanced Budget Act also established a National Bipartisan Commission on the Future of Medicare that was charged with making recommendations by March 1999 to "strengthen and improve" the Medicare system in time for the retirement of the baby boom generation. The 17-member commission failed to reach consensus on a single plan and, therefore, was unable to make any formal recommendations.

fully illustrated that relatively small changes in benefit formulas could substantially improve the financial position of the system and directing contributions to private retirement accounts would result in significant transition costs. Whether this will help trigger the broader reforms that are needed remains to be seen.

References

Congressional Budget Office (CBO), 2001a, *Budget Options* (Washington: U.S. Government Printing Office).

——, 2001b, *Social Security: A Primer* (Washington: U.S. Government Printing Office).

——, 2003, *The Budget and Economic Outlook: An Update* (Washington: U.S. Government Printing Office).

De Masi, P., and C. Towe, 2002, "Social Security, Medicare, and Long-Term U.S. Fiscal Prospects," in *United States: Selected Issues*, IMF Staff Country Report No. 02/165 (Washington: International Monetary Fund).

Diamond, P.A., and P.R. Orszag, 2002, "An Assessment of the Proposals of the President's Commission to Strengthen Social Security," NBER Working Paper No. 9097 (Cambridge, Massachusetts: National Bureau of Economic Research).

Gold, M., and L. Achman, 2003, "Average Out-of-Pocket Health Care Costs for Medicare+Choice Enrollees Increase 10 Percent in 2003," Issue Brief (New York: Commonwealth Fund).

Kohl, R., and P. O'Brien, 1998, "The Macroeconomics of Ageing, Pensions, and Savings: A Survey," OECD Economics Department Working Paper No. 200 (Paris: OECD).

Medicare Payment Advisory Commission, 2002, "Comparing Medicare and Private Sector Payment Rates for Physicians Services," Meeting Brief (Washington). Available via Internet: www.medpac.gov.

Medicare Trustees (Board of Trustees, Hospital Insurance and Supplementary Medical Insurance Trust Funds), 2003, *Annual Report* (Washington: U.S. Government Printing Office).

OASDI Trustees (Board of Trustees, Old-Age, Survivors, and Disability Insurance Trust Funds), 2003, *Annual Report* (Washington: U.S. Government Printing Office).

Organization for Economic Cooperation and Development (OECD), 2001, *OECD Economic Outlook*, Vol. 2001/1, No. 69 (Paris: OECD).

Social Security Commission, President's Commission to Strengthen Social Security, 2001, "Strengthening Social Security and Creating Personal Wealth for All Americans," December 21. Available via Internet: www.csss.gov/reports/Final_report.pdf.

IV Long-Run U.S. Fiscal Imbalance: An Intergenerational Analysis

Roberto Cardarelli and Christopher Towe

The recent dramatic deterioration of the U.S. fiscal position has heightened long-standing concerns about the extent to which the retirement and health care systems are prepared to cope with the pressures of an aging population. These concerns have been echoed in the administration's FY2004 budget, which described these programs as being on "an unsustainable path" and stated that the "resources of these programs are insufficient to cover their long-range shortfalls."[1]

The insolvency of the Social Security and Medicare programs is not a new phenomenon. It has been highlighted on a regular basis in the annual reports of the Old Age, Survivors, and Disability Insurance (OASDI) and Medicare Trustees, with the 2003 reports suggesting that the combined actuarial deficit of these programs is in the range of 160 percent of current GDP, if calculated over a 75-year horizon.[2]

More recent analysis, however, has flagged that actuarial estimates, which tend to focus only on the Social Security and Medicare systems, may provide a misleading picture of the effect of demographics on the broader fiscal imbalance. For example, Auerbach, Gale, and Orszag (2003) illustrate that, at least to some degree, tax revenues may be boosted by withdrawals from tax-deferred instruments by retirees. Similarly, OECD's (2001) analysis has shown that estimates of the fiscal impact of population aging also needs to take into account the full gamut of age-related spending, including on education, which may partly offset the rise in spending on the elderly.

At the same time, these broader analyses also suggest that the standard actuarial estimates of the Social Security and Medicare imbalances tend to offer too optimistic an assessment of the fiscal imbalance, while obscuring the intergenerational inequities involved. For example, the 75-year horizon used in assessing the position of the OASDI system would

suggest that the payroll tax increase required to "balance the system" would be only 1.87 percentage points. However, while such a tax hike would meet the system's obligations over the next 75 years, in net present value terms, it would still leave a significant cash flow deficit at the end of the period. Moreover, closing the fiscal gap can be accomplished through a variety of instruments (e.g., tax hikes, spending cuts, and so on) and in varying degrees of urgency (e.g., immediate tax hikes, or tax hikes phased in over years or decades). These alternatives have significantly different implications for the economic well-being of different generations, which are not captured by typical actuarial measures.

These considerations have led to a renewed emphasis on fiscal gap estimates that take into account longer horizons and the intergenerational transfers that are involved. Most recently, Gokhale and Smetters (2003) have prepared estimates of the U.S. fiscal imbalance using an intergenerational accounting framework that encompasses the entire federal fiscal system over an infinite horizon. Their results are alarming, suggesting that the U.S. fiscal imbalance is over 400 percent of current GDP (or 6.5 percent of the present value of future GDP), and that filling this fiscal gap would require measures that yield a 70 percent immediate and permanent increase in personal and corporate income tax revenues—that is, the ratio of GDP to federal income tax would have to be raised from just under 10 percent at present to 16 percent.

In this section, these worrisome conclusions are confirmed by constructing similar estimates of the U.S. intergenerational fiscal accounts. The results presented below suggest that the fiscal imbalance is as high as $47 trillion, nearly 500 percent of current GDP, and that closing this fiscal gap would require an immediate and permanent 60 percent hike in the federal income tax yield, or a 50 percent cut in Social Security and Medicare benefits. The analysis also illustrates that this gap is associated with a severe intergenerational imbalance—the burden that future generations will be required to bear to close this fiscal gap will be significant and will only increase further if measures are delayed.

---

[1]See U.S. Government (2003), Chapter 3.
[2]See OASDI Trustees (2003) and Medicare Trustees (2003).

Constructing Intergenerational Fiscal Accounts

The estimates are based on an intergenerational accounting framework, similar to that used by Gokhale and Smetters (2003). This approach first requires an estimate of the distribution of taxes and transfers across age cohorts in the current year.[3] Long-term fiscal projections are then constructed by assuming that taxes and transfers paid, and the level of other government outlays received, by the average person in each age cohort increase in line with productivity, unless programmatic or policy commitments dictate a different growth path.[4]

The demographic projections used in the baseline scenario are derived from the intermediate series of the 2003 OASDI Trustees' report, which represent the Social Security Administration's (SSA's) best estimate of future demographic trends. The projections cover the period 2002–80 and are extended beyond this horizon by using the SSA's terminal year fertility, mortality, and immigration assumptions.[5] During the next 10 years, the age distribution of the U.S. population is expected to remain roughly unchanged. After 2010, however, the old-age dependency ratio (the ratio of retirees to those in the labor force) begins to increase rapidly from around 20 percent in 2010 to 37 percent in 2036, stabilizing at around 40 percent after 2050. Labor productivity (defined as real GDP per hour worked) is assumed to grow at a rate of 1.7 percent per year. This rate equals the average annual rate achieved by the U.S. economy over the past 40 years and is in line with the assumption used by Gokhale and Smetters (2003) and the intermediate assumption in the 2003 OASDI Trustees' report.

During 2002–08, federal revenues are projected to grow in line with the estimates contained in the July 2003 Mid-Session Review of the FY2004 budget. During 2008–75, revenues from payroll tax contributions and premiums to the Social Security and Medicare trust funds are derived from the intermediate projections contained in the 2003 OASDI and Medicare Trustees' reports. All other revenues, including Social Security and Medicare revenues after 2075, are projected by assuming that per capita taxes and contributions increase in line with labor productivity, taking into account the impact of projected shifts in the age and gender distribution of the population.[6]

The simulations implicitly assume, therefore, that the tax cuts of recent years are made permanent, in line with the stated policy of the administration. In the long run, the ratio of tax revenues to GDP evolves in response to changes in the composition of the population. For example, revenues from individual income taxes attributed to labor are projected to remain constant as a share of output, as both these revenues and GDP are affected by the decline of the working-age population. Conversely, revenues from taxes on nonlabor income increase as a proportion of GDP because of the increase in the elderly population relative to those in the working-age cohorts (Figure 4.1).[7] Relative to GDP, Social Security contributions decline slightly, as taxable payrolls decline as a share of GDP.

During 2002–08, federal outlays are derived from the estimates contained in the Mid-Session Review of the FY2004 budget. After 2008, both discretionary and mandatory outlays are projected assuming that per capita spending, on an age- and gender-adjusted basis, grows in line with labor productivity.[8] The exception is spending on Social Security and

---

[3]For another example of how this approach was applied to the United States, see the Congressional Budget Office's study on the long-term fiscal outlook (CBO, 2000).

[4]These projections do not incorporate any feedback between the fiscal position and macroeconomic variables, such as productivity growth or interest rates. Therefore, they simply provide an indication of the magnitude of long term pressures for fiscal balances if current tax and spending policies remained unchanged, given long-term economic and demographic assumptions.

[5]Under the intermediate projections, the total fertility rate is assumed to gradually decline from the estimated level of 2.05 in 2001 to the long-term rate of 1.95 by 2027; life expectancy at birth is assumed to rise from 74.2 in 2002 to 81.6 in 2080 for men, and from 79.5 to 85.5 for women; and total level of net immigration (both legal and illegal) is assumed to decline gradually from the estimated level of 1.2 million persons in 2002 to 900,000 persons in 2023 and for each year afterward.

[6]The gender and age distribution of tax payments is calculated on the basis of data from several sources, including the Current Population Survey and the Survey of Consumer Finances. Social Security and Medicare future outlays and revenues are expressed in 2002 dollars by using the projections of the consumer price index for urban wage earners and clerical workers (CPI-W) contained in the 2003 report of the OASDI Trustees.

[7]Taxes on labor are the labor income part of the individual income tax revenues. This is estimated based on the average share of labor income in net national income over the last 10 years. Taxes on capital are the capital plus corporate income part of individual income tax revenues. These revenues are allocated across cohorts based on the age profile of wealth, which is skewed toward older cohorts.

[8]The gender and age distribution of outlays, as above, is estimated on the basis of various sources. Note that the expenditure projections deviate from a strict "current policy" assumption, since many noncontributory income security transfers—including income support, food stamps, aid to families with dependent children—are at present indexed only to CPI inflation. However, assuming CPI indexation over the long run implies that these payments would decline steadily as a share of GDP per capita, which is unrealistic and inconsistent with past experience in which ad hoc increases in the benefit rates have been introduced. A similar strategy has been followed by the CBO (2000), which terms the policy assumption in its baseline projections as "prevailing," rather than "current."

Figure 4.1. Tax Revenues
(In percent of GDP)

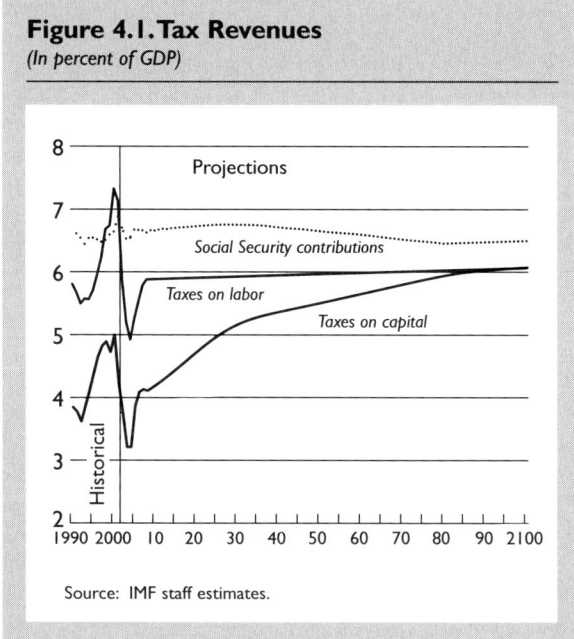

Source: IMF staff estimates.

Medicare, which is assumed to grow during 2008–80 in line with the intermediate projections contained in the 2003 OASDI and Medicare Trustees' reports. These reports have Medicare expenditure growing rapidly—at an average annual rate of 6½ percent in nominal terms—until 2012, reflecting recent trends and the impact of specific statutory provisions. During 2012–25, the Trustees' reports have Medicare expenditure growth slowing somewhat and after 2025, age- and gender-adjusted, per beneficiary expenditure increases 1 percent faster than labor productivity, reflecting continued shift in the relative price of health care.[9] To calculate the estimates described below, health care costs after 2080 are assumed to rise in line with productivity so that, after this year, changes in Medicare spending as a share of GDP reflect only a change in the demographic composition of the population.[10]

[9]This assumption is aimed at capturing the fact that historically per capita health expenditure has increased significantly more than wages, as a result of the increase in the utilization and complexity of health services. Deflating nominal outlays using the CPI yields that real spending on Medicare has grown at an average annual 4¾ percent between 1990 and 2002, almost 2 percentage points faster than real GDP. Such a pace is higher than the one assumed in the simulations, as the projections in the Medicare Trustees' report imply an average growth rate of real spending on Medicare of about 3½ percent for the period 2002–75.

[10]Spending on Medicaid is assumed to grow during 2008–80, based on the Medicare long-term assumption that age- and gender-adjusted, per beneficiary expenditure will increase at a rate of 1 percent faster than labor productivity. Again, this assumption appears more conservative than historical experience suggests. While real spending on Medicaid has grown annually at an aver-

Based on these assumptions, spending on Social Security is projected to accelerate rapidly from about 2010 to 2030 as the baby boom generation reaches retirement age, rising from 4½ percent of GDP in 2002 to around 7 percent of GDP in 2080 (Figure 4.2). Spending on Medicare (net of premiums) is also projected to increase rapidly, from around 2¼ percent of GDP in 2002 to 5¼ percent of GDP in 2035 and to around 9 percent of GDP in 2080 (Figure 4.3).

To illustrate the sensitivity of the projections to assumptions regarding the Medicare system for the longer-term solvency of the federal budget, an alternative scenario is constructed that assumes that the 1 percentage point gap between health care costs and productivity growth is eliminated from 2008 onward. In this case, Medicare spending as a share of GDP would increase only as a result of shifts in the age distribution of the population, rising to only around 5¾ percent by 2080.

Using the projected path for revenues and expenditures, the fiscal primary balance, debt service costs, and the change in the net debt of the government sector (gross federal debt held by the public less federal government financial assets) are then calculated.[11]

age of 8½ percent between 1990 and 2002, based on the above assumption it is projected to grow at an average annual rate of 3¾ percent during 2008–75.

[11]For the present calculations, the effective nominal interest rate on net government debt is assumed to be constant at 4.7 percent, which is equal to the average annual effective interest rate projected by the FY2004 budget for 2002–08.

Figure 4.2. Social Transfers
(In percent of GDP)

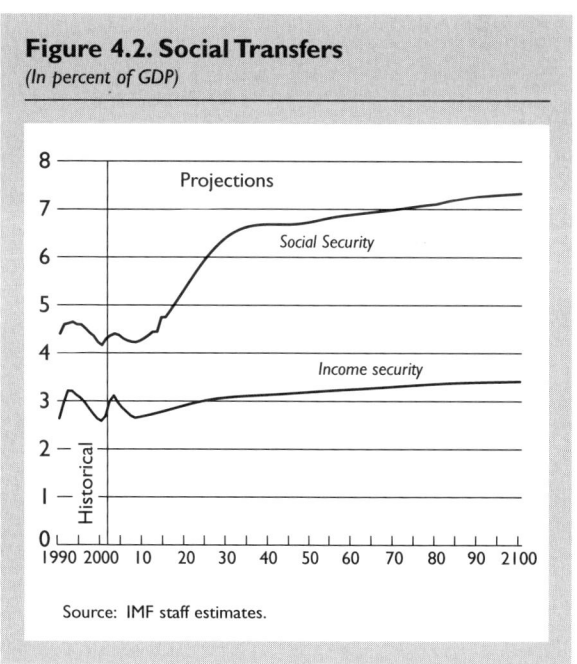

Source: IMF staff estimates.

Figure 4.3. Health Care Spending
(In percent of GDP)

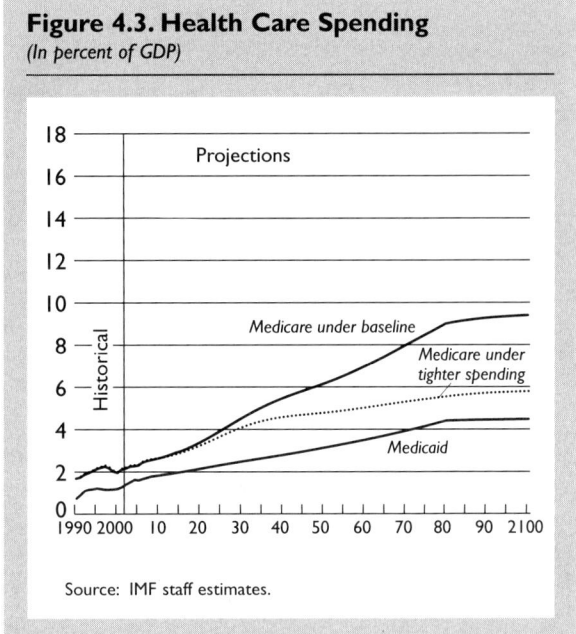

Source: IMF staff estimates.

Debt Dynamics and Fiscal Sustainability

In this section, we present the implications of these assumptions for various indices of the long-term fiscal position, including the standard debt- and deficit-to-GDP ratios, as well as measures of the fiscal imbalance and the fiscal gap. The fiscal imbalance represents the net present value of future government revenues less noninterest expenditures and current government net debt, and it is roughly equivalent to the government's actuarial balance.[12] The fiscal gap is a calculation of the immediate increase in income taxes that would be required to close the intertemporal budget imbalance.[13]

The long-term fiscal projections that are derived from these assumptions confirm the perilous situation facing the U.S. economy. As earlier studies have illustrated, the effect of demographic pressures on both retirement and health care systems, as well as the rapid increase in the price of health care services, would cause government debt and deficits to explode over the next century. In this case, the primary deficit rises sharply and reaches nearly 11½ percent of GDP by 2080, with government debt exceeding 600 percent of GDP by 2080 (Table 4.1).

These estimates suggest that U.S. federal government faces an intertemporal deficit of $47 trillion, nearly five times the present level of U.S. GDP (Table 4.2). Social Security transfers (net of payroll

---

[12]In calculating the present values of future receipts and outlays, the baseline scenario assumes a discount rate of 3.6 percent, which is the average real yield on 30-year Treasury bonds in recent years, as in Gokhale and Smetters (2003).

[13]It is thus different than a common interpretation given to the "fiscal gap" measure, namely, the immediate increase in taxes and/or decrease in spending necessary to assure that the debt-to-GDP ratio would return to the initial level by a certain time period. Clearly, restricting the analysis to a finite horizon period would not provide a complete picture of the long-run soundness of the federal budget if the overall fiscal balance continued to worsen at the end of the period.

Table 4.1. Long-Term Projections as a Share of GDP

	2002	2008	2020	2030	2040	2060	2080
Social Security	4.4	4.2	5.4	6.4	6.7	6.9	7.1
Old-age and survivors insurance	3.7	3.5	4.5	5.4	5.6	5.7	5.9
Disability insurance	0.6	0.7	0.9	1.1	1.1	1.2	1.2
Medicare	2.2	2.6	3.4	4.6	5.5	7.0	9.0
Part A	1.4	1.8	2.2	3.0	3.7	4.9	6.6
Part B	1.0	0.8	1.2	1.6	1.8	2.1	2.5
Medicaid	1.4	1.8	2.2	2.5	2.8	3.5	4.4
Other expenditure	9.6	9.0	9.6	10.1	10.3	10.6	10.9
Total expenditure	17.6	17.6	20.6	23.6	25.3	28.0	31.4
Total revenues	17.7	17.9	18.7	19.3	19.5	19.7	20.0
Primary balance	0.1	0.2	−1.9	−4.3	−5.8	−8.3	−11.5
Net interests	1.6	1.9	2.0	3.7	6.4	14.5	27.3
Overall balance	−1.5	−1.6	−4.0	−8.0	−12.2	−22.8	−38.8
Net debt[1]	28.4	35.2	47.4	86.0	147.7	331.3	620.3

Sources: OMB, *Mid-Session Review, Budget of U.S. Government, FY2004* (July 2003); OSADI 2003 Trustees' report; and IMF staff estimates.
[1]Net financial debt at the end of FY2001 (debt held by the public less federal government financial assets) (U.S. Government, 2003, Table 3.1, p. 37).

Table 4.2. Indicators of Fiscal Imbalance in Alternative Economic and Policy Scenarios

	Fiscal Imbalance (in trillions of U.S. dollars)	Increase in Income Taxes for All Generations That Closes the Imbalance (in percent)	Decrease in Social Security and Medicare Benefits for All Generations That Closes the Imbalance (in percent)
Baseline	47.2	61.1	−53.4
Demographic projections: low-cost scenario	47.5	53.0	−51.0
Higher productivity (2 percent)	61.1	66.0	−55.3
Higher productivity (2 percent) and no commensurate increase in expenditure[1]	33.6	36.3	−38.0
Tighter Medicare spending[2]	28.8	37.4	−37.8
Noncontributory transfers and government expenditure indexed to prices[3]	7.8	10.1	−9.5
Adjustment delayed to 2010	47.2	67.9	−57.1
Adjustment delayed to 2020	47.2	82.2	−63.7

Sources: OMB, *Mid-Session Review, Budget of U.S. Government, FY2004* (July 2003); OASDI 2003 Trustees' report; and IMF staff estimates.

[1]Per capita revenues from income tax, excise tax, and custom tax rise at 2 percent per annum compared with 1.7 percent in the baseline scenario, while all other revenues and expenditure remain unchanged.

[2]Medicare and Medicaid transfers per capita grow at the same rate as labor productivity from 2008 onward.

[3]All federal consumption and noncontributory transfers per capita are indexed to prices only.

contributions) account for a third of the imbalance, while Medicare transfers (net of payroll taxes and premium payments by the elderly) account for the remaining two-thirds, with the rest of the federal government showing a small surplus. Closing this fiscal gap would require a 60 percent immediate and permanent increase in personal and corporate income tax revenues or, alternatively, an immediate and permanent 50 percent cut in Social Security and Medicare outlays.[14] By comparison, the tax cuts enacted since early 2001—if assumed permanent—have lowered the income tax ratio by about 15 percent, implying that the tax cuts have expanded the fiscal gap by roughly one-third.

Correcting this fiscal imbalance will involve a substantial intergenerational redistribution of wealth that will only be magnified if the adjustment is

[14]These estimates are much larger than the 75-year period actuarial imbalances reported by the SSA, for the reasons explained in footnote 13, but are broadly consistent with the $44 trillion estimate of the fiscal imbalance prepared by Gokhale and Smetters (2003). Differences between the Gokhale and Smetters estimates and those described above may reflect the weakening of the longer-term fiscal position that has occurred during 2003 and different assumptions regarding the extension of the normal retirement age.

delayed.[15] For example, if the adjustment is postponed until 2010, income tax revenues would have to increase by nearly 70 percent relative to baseline, while deferring adjustment until 2020 would require an increase of over 80 percent. The size of the expenditure adjustment would similarly increase if the adjustment were delayed. The larger adjustment that would be required in later years would mean that a greater proportion of tax increases (or expenditure cuts) would have to be borne by younger workers or those not yet in the workforce, while the burden faced by the current elderly, and others in the workforce, would be correspondingly lessened.

[15]One way to illustrate this redistribution is to compare the present value of the net lifetime taxes paid by a person born in the current year versus the taxes that would have to be paid by future generations, assuming that the burden of adjustment is borne by these future generations. The estimates suggest that this gap—in present value terms—would be around $270,000. In other words, future generations would have to pay almost twice as much income tax during their lifetimes than those alive at present, compared with a 60 percent increase in tax burdens that would be required if the increase applied to all generations immediately. A similar redistribution would occur if the adjustment takes place on the expenditure side. See Cardarelli, Sefton, and Kotlikoff (2000); and Gokhale and Smetters (2003) for a discussion of alternative indicators of intergenerational fiscal equity.

The results mentioned above, while alarming, appear relatively robust in the face of alternative economic and policy assumptions. Alternative demographic projections do not significantly affect the broad picture that emerges—for example, using the SSA's low-cost alternative, which embodies a higher fertility rate, slower improvements in mortality, and higher immigration flows, still yields a large imbalance. Similarly, higher productivity growth does not improve the fiscal imbalance, principally because retirement and health care spending are assumed to increase commensurately.

At the same time, measures to contain the growth of spending can significantly improve the fiscal imbalance. Simply containing Medicare spending to the rate of productivity growth lowers the gap to $28 trillion and roughly halves the immediate and permanent increase in income tax revenues required. Substantial reductions in the imbalance are also obtained if noncontributory transfers and federal consumption expenditure are indexed only to prices, rather than to real wages and/or productivity growth (see Table 4.2).

Conclusions

As noted in the introduction to this section, the results above underscore the well-known point that demographic and cost pressures on health care programs will—in the absence of policy measures—place an enormous burden on the U.S. federal budget. The specific estimates above suggest a fiscal gap of $47 trillion, or nearly 500 percent of current GDP. Closing this gap would require massive adjustments in either tax or spending programs. The longer-term fiscal deficit is also associated with a severe intergenerational imbalance; the estimates clearly illustrate that the longer the action is delayed, the greater will be the adjustment required and larger the burden that will be placed on future generations.

Although these results are undeniably worrisome, the discussion above suggests that the U.S. fiscal problem is manageable if action is taken soon. Most importantly, early steps to contain the growth of spending on entitlement programs, by enacting reforms to slow the growth of Medicare spending and contain the projected growth of Social Security benefits, would significantly narrow the fiscal gap. In the absence of action on these fronts, significant tax measures may be required, including a willingness to allow the cuts of recent years to expire as scheduled.

References

Auerbach, A.J., W.G. Gale, and P.R. Orszag, 2003, "Reassessing the Fiscal Gap: Why Tax-Deferred Saving Will Not Solve the Problem," *Tax Notes* (Washington: Urban Institute, Brookings Institution), July 28.

Congressional Budget Office (CBO), 2000, *The Long-Term Budget Outlook* (Washington: U.S. Government Printing Office).

Gokhale, J., and K. Smetters, 2003, *Fiscal and Generational Imbalances: New Budget Measures for New Budget Priorities* (Washington: AEI Press).

Cardarelli, R., J. Sefton, and L.J. Kotlikoff, 2000, "Generational Accounting in the U.K.," *Economic Journal*, Vol. 110, No. 467, pp. 547–74.

Medicare Trustees (Board of Trustees, Hospital Insurance and Federal Supplementary Medical Insurance Trust Funds), 2003, *Annual Report* (Washington: U.S. Government Printing Office).

OASDI Trustees (Board of Trustees, Old-Age, Survivors, and Disability Insurance Trust Funds), 2003, *Annual Report* (Washington: U.S. Government Printing Office).

Office of Management and Budget, 2003, *Mid-Session Review, Fiscal Year 2004* (Washington: U.S. Government Printing Office), July.

Organization for Economic Cooperation and Development (OECD), 2001, *OECD Economic Surveys: United States* (Paris: OECD).

U.S. Government, 2003, *Budget of the United States Government, Fiscal Year 2004: Analytical Perspectives* (Washington: U.S. Government Printing Office).

V U.S. Energy Policy: Role of Taxation

Jim Prust and Dominique Simard

Following the release of the administration's National Energy Policy in 2001, far-reaching energy legislation is being considered in Congress.[1] The legislation seems to be mainly driven by two issues: the security-related and macroeconomic risks stemming from U.S. dependence on oil imports and a recognition of the environmental consequences, including greenhouse gas emissions, of the energy intensity of the U.S. economy.

None of the initiatives has emphasized taxes as a means of discouraging energy consumption. The focus, instead, has been on measures geared toward boosting domestic energy supply and developing new technologies to increase the efficiency of energy use. Tax proposals have been limited to providing tax subsidies for domestic energy production as well as developing energy-efficient production processes, at a substantial fiscal cost. This section suggests that there may be a case for considering consumption-based energy taxes to meet both energy and fiscal policy objectives.

Energy Use in the United States

Although declining, the energy intensity of GDP in the United States remains well above that in most other industrial countries (Figure 5.1). As in many other industrialized countries, the energy intensity of GDP in the United States has fallen steadily during the last half century. The drop in energy intensity, measured in British thermal units (Btu) per real dollar of GDP, was particularly rapid from the 1970s through the mid-1980s, when real energy prices were above their historical average (Figure 5.2). More recently, the decline has accelerated again, partly reflecting a structural shift away from manufacturing and toward a more information technology–intensive economy (EIA, 2003). Nevertheless, U.S. consumption remains 30–50 percent higher per unit of GDP than in Europe.[2]

The higher energy intensity of the United States partly reflects geographic and tax-related factors. To a significant degree, energy usage in both the United States and Canada has reflected the need to cope with low population densities and relatively severe and variable climate conditions compared with Europe.[3] However, energy prices in the United States are also significantly lower than in most other industrial countries. For example, average U.S. gasoline prices in 2001 were more than 50 percent below European prices and 10–15 percent lower than Cana-

---

[3]The main user of energy in the United States in 2001 was the industrial sector (33 percent of total Btu consumption), followed by the transportation sector (28 percent), the residential sector (21 percent), and the commercial sector (18 percent). Canada's high level of energy intensity also reflects the preponderance of energy-intensive industry.

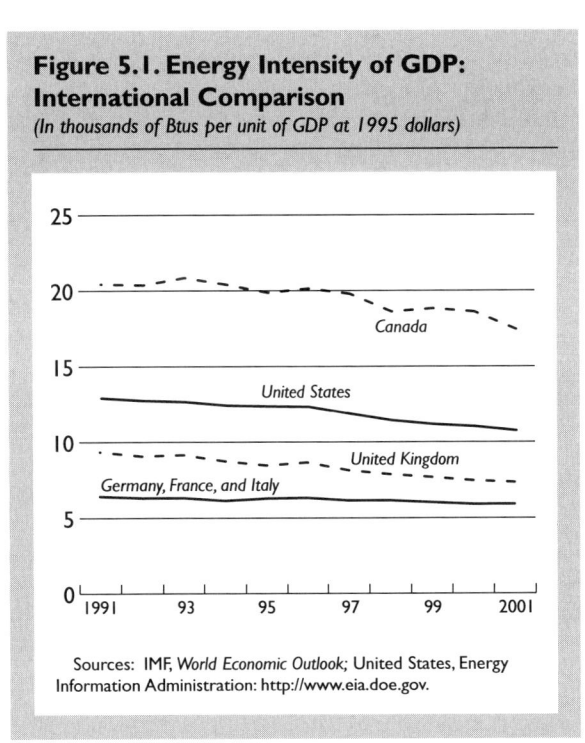

Figure 5.1. Energy Intensity of GDP: International Comparison
(In thousands of Btus per unit of GDP at 1995 dollars)

Sources: IMF, *World Economic Outlook;* United States, Energy Information Administration: http://www.eia.doe.gov.

---

[1]Benjamin Hunt prepared the simulations presented in this section.

[2]Japan was omitted from the group of comparable countries because of its vastly different geography and land use patterns.

Figure 5.2. Energy Intensity of GDP and Real Motor Gasoline Price
(In dollars per million Btu)

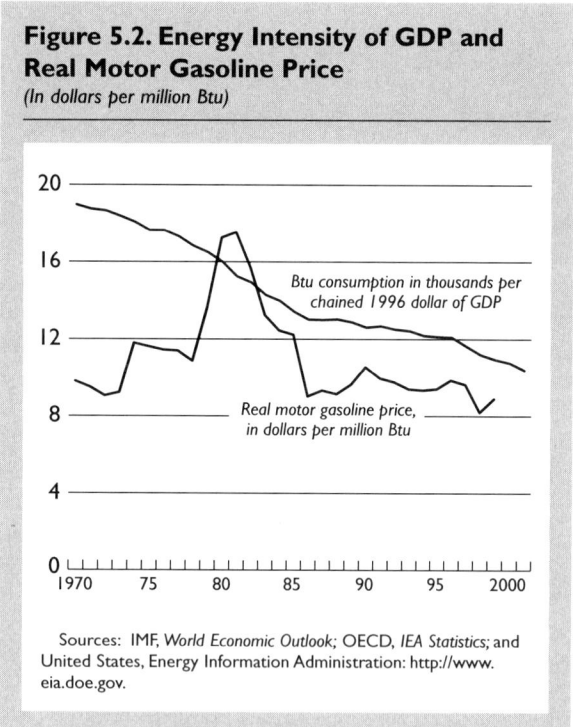

Sources: IMF, *World Economic Outlook*; OECD, *IEA Statistics*; and United States, Energy Information Administration: http://www.eia.doe.gov.

Figure 5.3. Real Prices of Premium Unleaded Gasoline
(Gasoline price, in 1996 U.S. dollars per liter)

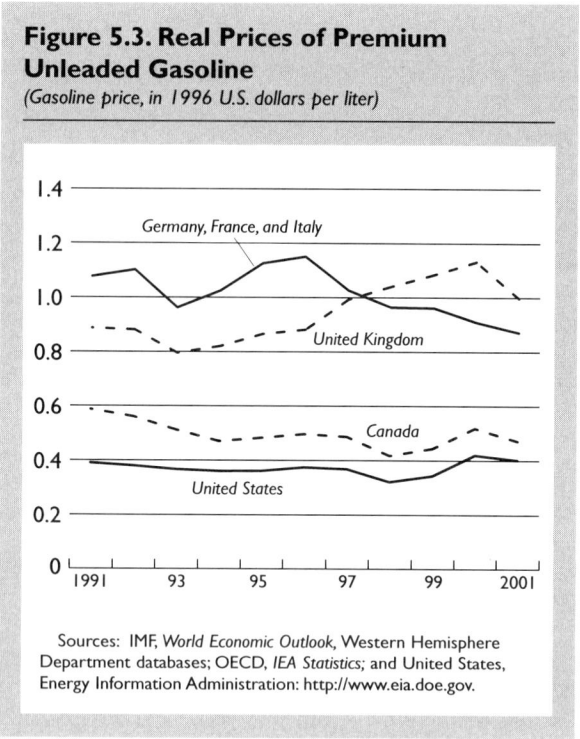

Sources: IMF, *World Economic Outlook*, Western Hemisphere Department databases; OECD, *IEA Statistics*; and United States, Energy Information Administration: http://www.eia.doe.gov.

Figure 5.4. Prices and Taxes of Premium Unleaded Gasoline
(In U.S. dollars per liter, 2001)

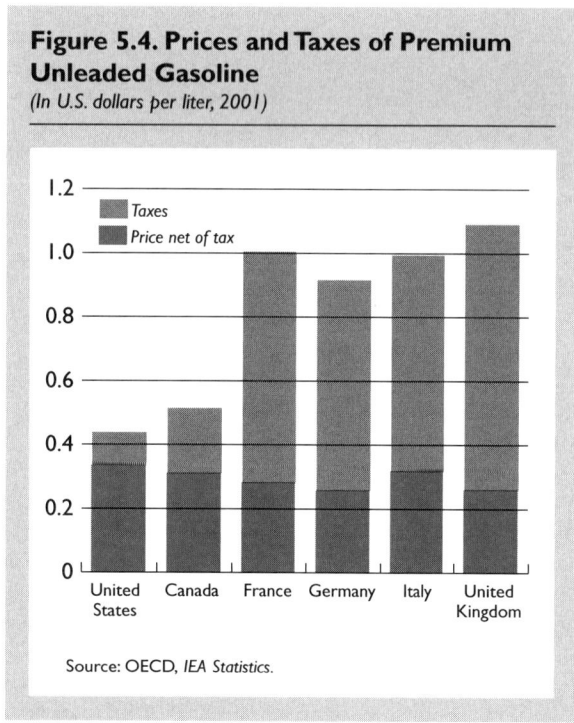

Source: OECD, *IEA Statistics*.

Figure 5.5. Carbon Dioxide Emissions per GDP
(In metric tons equivalent per thousand 1995 U.S. dollars)

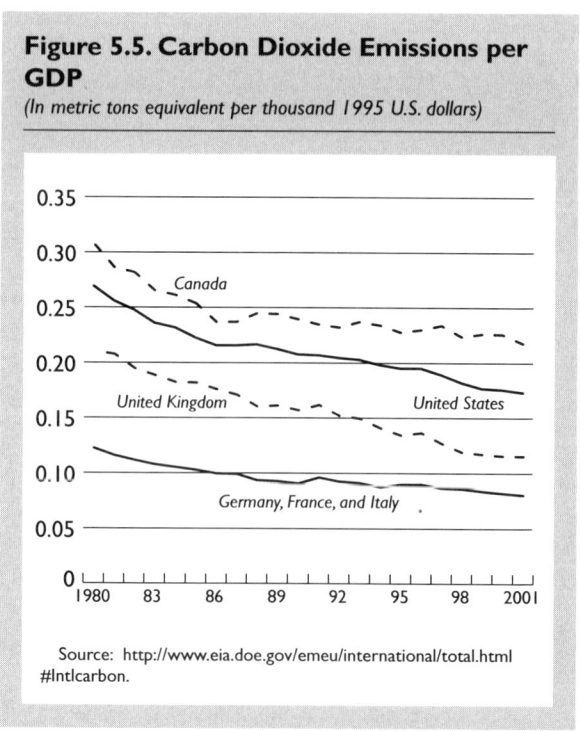

Source: http://www.eia.doe.gov/emeu/international/total.html #Intlcarbon.

dian prices (Figure 5.3), with the difference mostly accounted for by taxation (Figure 5.4). The prices of most other energy products—for example, electricity and natural gas—display similar cross-country variation.[4]

High U.S. energy intensity has been associated with greenhouse gas (GHG) emissions that are among the highest per unit of GDP of major industrialized countries (Figure 5.5). International rankings of emissions of carbon dioxide (CO_2)—the principal GHG—are broadly consistent with the energy intensity of GDP, notwithstanding differences in countries' reliance on fossil fuels, and differences in the carbon content of different fuels.

Hydrocarbons represent the principal source of U.S. energy (Figure 5.6). The share of energy consumption from petroleum fell from a peak of nearly 50 percent in the mid-1970s to around 40 percent by the end of the 1990s. The share of natural gas peaked at 32 percent in 1970 and now stands at around 25

percent—roughly the same share as coal, which remains the main source of fuel for electricity generation. Although the share of energy produced from nuclear, hydroelectric, and other nonfossil fuel sources has increased since 1973, it remains at just under 15 percent of total consumption.

Petroleum imports have been rising steadily since the mid-1980s (Figure 5.7). Net imports of petroleum are projected by the U.S. Department of Energy to continue to grow strongly for the next quarter century, and the share of net imports in total U.S. petroleum consumption is expected to increase from 55 percent in 2001 to 68 percent in 2025.

Energy Policy

The U.S. administration's National Energy Policy (NEP) was released in May 2001. The NEP's principal focus is on addressing the "fundamental imbalance between supply and demand" and the projected increase in U.S. dependence on energy imports (NEPDG, 2001). Specific policy measures focused on promoting "dependable, affordable, and environmentally sound production and distribution of energy" and include

- subsidies to promote conservation by households;

- funding for research and development into alternative energy sources;

---

[4]According to International Energy Agency statistics, this observation is robust across different years (IEA, 2003). Products with homogeneous net-of-tax prices across countries, such as gasoline and diesel, display a wide cross-country variation of end-user prices because of different tax policy choices. Other products, which are less easily traded internationally, such as electricity and natural gas, display a wider international variation in their net-of-tax prices. For example, Canadian prices of natural gas and electricity have in the past tended to be lower than in the United States, reflecting their relatively abundant supply in Canada, including from hydroelectric generation. However, taxes on these products also differ across countries.

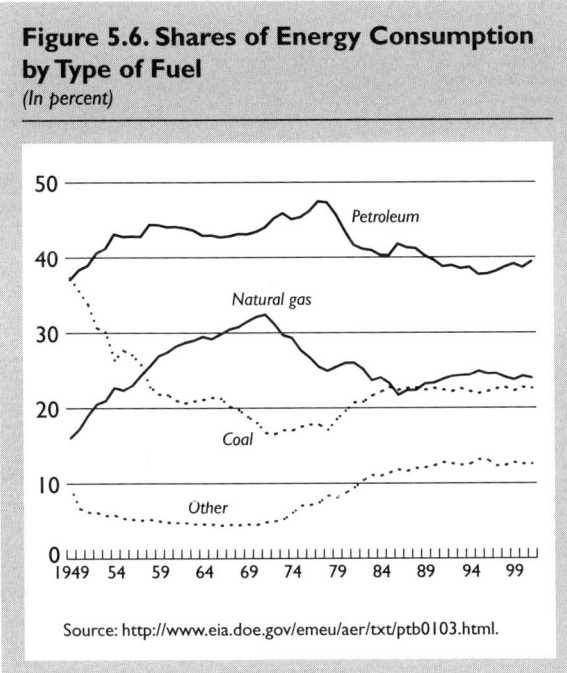

Figure 5.6. Shares of Energy Consumption by Type of Fuel
(In percent)

Source: http://www.eia.doe.gov/emeu/aer/txt/ptb0103.html.

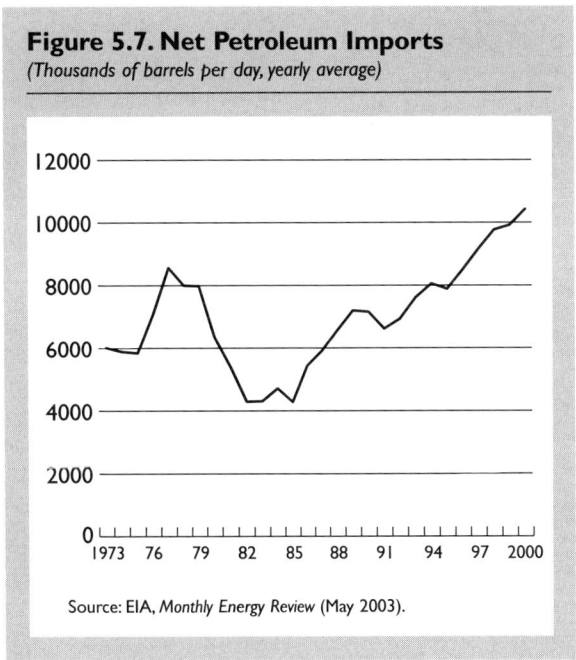

Figure 5.7. Net Petroleum Imports
(Thousands of barrels per day, yearly average)

Source: EIA, *Monthly Energy Review* (May 2003).

- establishing a new regulatory structure for the electricity sector, including the extension of the tradable emissions permit system on sulphur dioxide and introducing similar systems for emissions of nitrogen oxides (NO_x) and mercury;

- revising emissions standards for autos and household appliances;

- tax credits to encourage the use of fuel-efficient vehicles, new landfill methane projects, electricity produced from wind and biomass, residential solar energy property, and the purchase of new hybrid or fuel-cell vehicles; and

- opening the Arctic National Wildlife Reserve (ANWR) for oil exploration and pipelines, and earmarking associated royalties for conservation.

The NEP has helped shape energy legislation subsequently debated by Congress. Its major provisions include loan guarantees and tax credits for pipeline development; tax breaks for oil, gas, and coal industries; tax incentives for improving energy of homes and appliances, and for encouraging development and use of renewable energy sources, including biomass and waste; and a mandated increase of the use of ethanol in gasoline.

The administration's environmental policy proposals have potentially important implications for the energy sector. In 2001, the administration rejected the Kyoto Protocol, which would bind countries to targets for reducing GHG emissions. The decision reflected the administration's view that its goals were unrealistic and had potentially harmful implications for U.S. economic growth.[5] Instead, the administration proposed its Clear Skies Initiative in 2002. The centerpiece of the Initiative is a commitment to reducing, by 2012, the emission intensity—defined as GHG emissions relative to real output—in the United States by 18 percent.[6] This objective is to be met primarily through the combined effect of measures proposed by the administration, including an extension of existing cap-and-trade programs.

Significant cap-and-trade programs are already in place in the United States to reduce air pollutants. For example, under the Clean Air Act, electric utilities were allocated sulphur dioxide (SO_2) emissions allowances beginning in 1995 and allowed to buy and sell unused portions of these allowances as they saw

fit. A tradable permits program also exists for nitrogen oxide emissions in the eastern United States.

Taxation and Other Instruments to Reduce Energy Consumption

Many analysts have argued that energy taxes can play an important role in achieving conservation and environmental goals. Taxes are widely viewed as an effective instrument for restraining demand and encouraging efficient resource use, as well as for aligning private and social costs in the presence of externalities (Sandmo, 1976). Indeed, a range of tax instruments is already in place in the United States to address environmental, conservation, and fiscal objectives on both the federal and state levels (Box 5.1).

Alternative approaches to increasing energy efficiency—including direct regulation of energy use and subsidization of new technologies—have important drawbacks:

- For example, a study by the Congressional Budget Office—which compared the relative merits of Corporate Average Fuel Economy (CAFE) standards and similar regulatory approaches with gasoline taxes—found that taxes were considerably less costly from an economic efficiency perspective (CBO, 2002). Since CAFE standards did not directly target fuel-saving activities by the consumer, any given decrease in targeted gasoline consumption could be made at a lower cost through a gasoline tax (CBO, 2002).

- A similar point was made by Goulder and Schneider (1999), whose simulations illustrate that achieving a 10 percent reduction in carbon dioxide emissions would be 10 times more costly if technology subsidies were employed as a stand-alone measure, relative to a broader approach that combined technology subsidies with policies to raise the cost of carbon, such as tradable carbon permits or carbon taxes.

- Questions have also been raised regarding the efficiency of subsidizing both the development and introduction of new, fuel-efficient technologies, given the uncertainty inherent in choosing the technology that will yield significant payoffs (Sutherland, 1999).

What would be the optimal level of energy taxation in the United States? As emphasized by Bovenberg and Goulder (2002), economic theory suggests that optimal tax rates would be expected to vary across countries, based on the different costs that countries face regarding environmental degradation

---

[5]The United States, for example, would have to cut its GHG emissions by 7 percent, compared with 1990 levels, during 2008–12. Estimates have placed the cost of achieving this reduction as high as 2 percent of GDP.

[6]Goulder (2002) suggests that the administration's target would leave emissions roughly 10 percent higher than at the beginning of the decade and nearly 30 percent above the Kyoto Protocol target.

Box 5.1. U.S. Energy Excise Taxes

Federal Government

A large number of federal excises are levied on energy by the federal government. Fuel taxes average $0.184 per gallon, and estimates by the Joint Committee on Taxation and Internal Revenue Service indicate that federal fuel taxes yielded $29.6 billion (0.3 percent of GDP) in FY2003. The yield on other excises was smaller: for example, the excise tax on coal yielded $550 million, and the excise tax on the sale of automobiles with low fuel economy ratings yielded $78 million. The specific excises include

- Energy excise taxes for general revenue. These include
  —Tax of $0.43 per gallon rail diesel fuel and inland waterways fuel; $0.068 per gallon motorboat fuel, small engine gasoline, and special fuels.

- Excise taxes dedicated to environmental trust funds or designated funds. These include
  —Abandoned Mine Reclamation Fund: tax of $0.35 per ton of surface coal, $0.15 per ton of coal mined underground, $0.10 per ton of lignite (average tax estimated about $0.26 per ton in 1999).
  —Aquatic Resources Trust Fund: tax levied on motorboat gasoline and other fuel.
  —Highway Trust Fund: tax of $0.043 per gallon motor fuel.
  —Leaking Underground Storage Tank Trust Fund: tax of $0.001 per gallon motor fuel.
  —Nuclear Waste Fund: tax estimated to impose a 1.45 percent cost increment for power provided from nuclear energy in 1999.
  —Pipeline Safety Fund: user fees collected from pipeline operators.

—Uranium Enrichment Decontamination and Decommissioning Fund: contributions from commercial utilities based on historical enrichment services.

- Excise taxes dedicated to health-related trust funds. These include
  —Black Lung Disability Trust Fund: minimum of $0.55 per ton of coal or 4.4 percent of sales revenue if selling price is less than $25 per ton from surface mines or $12.50 per ton for surface coal.

- Excise tax on the sale of automobiles with relatively low fuel economy ratings. This includes
  —Tax ranging from $1,000 for an automobile rated between 21.5 and 22.5 miles per gallon (mpg) to $7,700 for an automobile rated at less than 12.5 mpg.

State Governments

All state and many local governments levy specific excise and sales taxes on fuel and other energy commodities. In 2002, excise taxes on motor fuel represented 6 percent of total taxes collected by states. Total state and local taxes on fuel varied from $0.08 per gallon in Alaska to $0.35 per gallon in New York. Many states also levy severance taxes—a tax on a portion of the value of the natural resource extracted—on oil, gas, and coal production. State energy severance taxes accounted for less than 0.8 percent of total state tax revenue in 2002.

Sources: EIA (1999); Lazzari (2003); U.S. Census Bureau (2003); and CBO (2002).

---

and remediation of environmental harm, opportunity cost of public funds, and political and administrative considerations. Similarly, two studies based on a representative agent model calibrated to the U.S. and U.K. economies have identified the key factors determining an optimal fuel tax (Parry, 2002; Parry and Small, 2002). These include, in decreasing order of importance, the social cost of automotive congestion, the capacity of the tax to raise revenue, and the extent to which fuel consumption imposes environmental externalities.

Although it is difficult to define the optimal level of energy taxation in practice, some studies suggest that energy taxes in the United States may be too low. Both the United States and Canada would be expected to impose relatively low taxes on diesel and gasoline, given their low population densities and congestion externalities relative to western European countries. Nonetheless, even adjusting for these con-

siderations, Parry (2002) and Parry and Small (2002) conclude that gasoline taxes in the United States may be only half their optimal level. In an earlier study, the OECD had not only suggested that an increase in fuel taxes of 40 cents per gallon could be justified given the range of externalities associated with road use, but also noted that roughly three-fourths of U.S. carbon emissions are not taxed at all (OECD, 2001a).

Recent U.S. and international experience has shown that tax measures can be usefully complemented by market-oriented regulatory approaches. For example, the cap-and-trade emissions permit system already in effect for SO_2 emissions has generally been viewed as a success (CBO, 2000). By limiting the quantity of permits, these systems can directly affect the level of emissions. However, a drawback of these approaches is that there is no upper limit to the costs that polluters may be obliged to incur to achieve given quantitative targets.

Approaches to deal with this problem include the facility to issue additional permits if permit prices exceed some ceiling and to grant a percentage of free permits instead of auctioning them (Goulder, 2002).

Macroeconomic Effects of Energy Taxation

The impact of energy taxation on demand and fiscal revenue depends importantly on the price elasticity of demand. Most studies suggest that energy demand is considerably more price elastic in the long run than in the short run. For example, short-run elasticities for energy and fuel demand are estimated in the range between –0.13 and –0.26, compared with long-run elasticities in the range between –0.37 and –0.46 (OECD, 2001b). A detailed survey of 97 econometric studies of the elasticity of demand for gasoline found that the short-run elasticity averaged –0.26, compared with an average long-run elasticity of –0.86 (Dahl and Sterner, 1991).

These findings suggest that taxes could have a substantial impact on consumption while, at the same time, raising significant government revenues. For example, the CBO estimates that a 15 cent per gallon hike in gasoline taxes could have raised $16 billion in additional budget revenue in 2003, more than doubling existing revenues (CBO, 2002). According to the OECD (2001a), a carbon tax of $100 per ton—equivalent in its effect on gasoline prices to a tax of about 30 cents per gallon—would have yielded $110 billion in 1999.

Concerns have been raised about the potential adverse impact of energy taxes on prices, real wages, and income distribution, but most studies show that the effects depend importantly on the use that is made of the additional tax revenue. For example, the adverse effects on output can be alleviated if the revenue is used to lower taxes on labor or investment (Bovenberg and Goulder, 1996; Nordhaus, 1993). Similarly, there is scope for addressing the impact on income distribution if revenues are used to compensate the population segments most vulnerable to tax

Table 5.1. Simulated Impact of Energy Taxes on the Economy
(Percent deviation from baseline)

	After One Year	After Five Years	Long Run
10 Percent Tax on Energy Used in Consumption			
Real GDP	–0.03	–0.02	–0.08
Consumption	–0.03	0.01	–0.04
Investment	–0.3	–0.3	–0.22
Consumption price of energy	7.69	8.33	9.38
Goods producers' price of energy	–2.09	–1.51	–0.56
Oil producers' price of energy	–2.59	–1.87	–0.67
Real exchange rate	0.16	0.23	0.22
10 Percent Tax on Energy Used in Production			
Real GDP	0.02	0.02	–0.03
Consumption	0.03	0.05	0
Investment	0	–0.01	–0.13
Consumption price of energy	–0.3	–1	–2.23
Goods producers' price of energy	9.67	8.91	7.62
Oil producers' price of energy	–0.38	–1.26	–2.79
Real exchange rate	0.12	0.11	0.26
10 Percent Tax on All Energy			
Real GDP	–0.01	–0.01	–0.11
Consumption	0.04	0.06	–0.04
Investment	–0.3	–0.32	–0.35
Consumption price of energy	7.39	7.27	7.02
Goods producers' price of energy	7.39	7.27	7.02
Oil producers' price of energy	–2.95	–3.09	–3.45
Real exchange rate	0.37	0.34	0.47

Source: IMF staff estimates.

increases, such as rural versus urban households (CBO, 2002).

Model Simulations

IMF staff simulations suggest that the output effects of higher energy taxes, which are redistributed to consumers, may be modest. A version of the IMF's Global Economy Model (GEM), calibrated to the U.S. economy, suggests that a 10 percentage point increase in taxes on petroleum products used as intermediate production inputs would reduce long-run U.S. GDP by 0.03 percent (Table 5.1).[7] A larger output loss—0.11 percent—would occur if the tax was also levied on the final consumption of petroleum products, reflecting the broader scope of the tax and the lower elasticity of substitution that applies to energy consumption.

These simulations take into account that the large size of the U.S. market influences the output effects of energy taxes. Part of the burden of higher U.S. taxes is shifted to the rest of the world through lower prices and an appreciated U.S. dollar because U.S. petroleum imports represent almost 20 percent of the world market. The simulations suggest that the short-run effects of a U.S. tax on energy used in production could even be positive because of different adjustment speeds of producer and consumer prices. The simulations also illustrate the importance of the elasticity of substitution—the higher the degree of substitutability between petroleum products and other goods and services, the more likely the domestic tax will cause world prices to fall and mitigate U.S. output declines. This exercise, however, does not take into account possible responses by world energy producers to the change in market conditions.

References

Bovenberg, A.L., and L.H. Goulder, 1996, "Optimal Environmental Taxation in the Presence of Other Taxes: General-Equilibrium Analysis," *American Economic Review*, Vol. 86, No. 4, pp. 985–1000.

———, 2002, "Environmental Taxation and Regulation," in *Handbook of Public Economics,* Vol. 3, edited by A. Auerbach and M. Feldstein (New York: Elsevier).

Congressional Budget Office (CBO), 2000, "Who Gains and Who Pays Under Carbon Allowance Trading? The Distributional Effects of Alternative Policy Designs," June.

———, 2002, "Reducing Gasoline Consumption: Three Policy Options," November.

Dahl, C., and T. Sterner, 1991, "Analyzing Gasoline Demand Elasticities: A Survey," *Energy Economics*, Vol. 13, No. 3, pp. 203–10.

Energy Information Administration (EIA), 1999, "Federal Energy Market Interventions 1999: Primary Energy" (Washington: EIA).

———, 2003, "Annual Energy Outlook 2003 with Projections to 2025" (Washington: EIA).

Environmental Protection Agency (EPA), 2003, "Clear Skies Act," February 27.

Goulder, L.H., 2002, "U.S. Climate-Change Policy: The Bush Administration's Plan and Beyond," Stanford Institute for Economic Policy Research Policy Brief (Palo Alto, California: Stanford University), February.

———, and S.L. Schneider (1999), "Induced Technological Change and the Attractiveness of CO_2 Emissions Abatement Policies," *Resource and Energy Economics*, Vol. 21, No. 3–4, pp. 211–53.

Hunt, B., 2003, "Oil Price Shocks: When Are They Bad and When Are They Not So Bad?" IMF Working Paper (Washington: International Monetary Fund), forthcoming.

International Energy Agency (IEA), 2003, *Energy Prices and Taxes*, various issues (Paris: OECD).

Lazzari, S., 2003, "Energy Tax Policy," Issue Brief for Congress, Congressional Research Service (Washington: Library of Congress).

National Energy Policy Development Group (NEPDG), 2001, "National Energy Policy," Washington.

Nordhaus, W.D., 1993, "Optimal Greenhouse-Gas Reductions and Tax Policy in the 'DICE' Model," *American Economic Review*, Vol. 83, No. 2, pp. 313–17.

Organization for Economic Cooperation Development (OECD), 2001a, *Economic Survey: United States* (Paris: OECD).

———, 2001b, *Environmentally Related Taxes in OECD Countries: Issues and Strategies* (Paris: OECD).

Parry, I., 2002, "Is Gasoline Undertaxed in the United States?" *Resources*, No. 148, pp. 28–33. Available via Internet: http://www.rff.org.

———, and K. Small, 2002, "Does Britain or the United States Have the Right Gasoline Tax?" Resources for the Future Discussion Paper No. 02–12 (Washington: Resources for the Future).

Pesenti, P., 2003, "The Global Economy Model (GEM): Theoretical Framework," IMF Working Paper (Washington: International Monetary Fund), forthcoming.

Sandmo, A., 1976, "Optimal Taxation: An Introduction to the Literature," *Journal of Public Economics*, Vol. 6, pp. 37–54.

Sutherland, R.J., 1999, "The Feasibility of 'No Cost' Efforts to Reduce Carbon Emissions in the U.S.," American Petroleum Institute (API) Issue Analysis No. 106 (Washington: API).

U.S. Census Bureau, 2003, "State Government Tax Collections: 2002" (Washington), April 22.

---

[7]The theoretical structure and derivation of the GEM can be found in Pesenti (2003), and an extension of the model fully incorporating the oil market is explained in Hunt (2003).

VI   Budget Enforcement Act and Options for Reform

Michael Kell

The elimination of the U.S. federal budget deficit during the 1990s marked a significant fiscal milestone at the time. The unified budget surplus in FY1998 was the first surplus in nearly 30 years, and surpluses in the following years were the largest relative to GDP since 1951 (Figure 6.1).[1]

Although the prolonged economic boom played a major role in turning the fiscal position around, a shift in the direction of policies was also instrumental. In particular, the 1990s were marked by a significant strengthening of budget discipline, codified in the 1990 Budget Enforcement Act (BEA). This legislation included strict caps on discretionary spending—that is, spending subject to annual appropriations—and a "pay-as-you-go" (PAYGO) requirement for new legislation affecting mandatory spending—that is, spending determined by permanent law—and tax receipts.

The recent deterioration in the fiscal position also appears to have reflected both cyclical and policy weaknesses. In addition to the effects of the collapse of the stock market, geopolitical events, and the onset of the 2001 recession, budget discipline weakened considerably, culminating in the expiration of the BEA at the end of FY2002. These developments, and the growing awareness of the need to reestablish a more sustainable fiscal position, have spurred questions about how, or whether, to reintroduce and reform budget enforcement procedures. This section discusses some of the principal reform options.

Background

Rising deficits during the 1980s prompted a series of reforms of budgetary legislation and procedures. Of these, the most significant were

- The Balanced Budget and Emergency Deficit Control Act of 1985, widely known as Gramm-Rudman-Hollings (GRH), which specified declining nominal targets for the deficit, culminating in a balanced budget in FY1991. Uniform

percentage cuts—termed sequestration—were supposed to be triggered in selected mandatory and most discretionary spending programs if the projected (rather than actual) deficits exceeded the targets.

- Faced with the prospect of huge spending cuts in 1987, Congress amended GRH by relaxing the deficit target and postponing a balanced budget until FY1993. These revised targets were never met, in part because of the financial burden associated with resolving the savings and loan crisis.

- The 1990 Budget Enforcement Act took a different approach by replacing the deficit targets of GRH with mechanisms to enforce agreed-upon levels of discretionary spending, and to ensure the budget neutrality of new spending and taxation laws (Box 6.1). The original Act covered FY1991–FY1995, but it was extended in 1993 and 1997 and remained in force until its expiration at the end of FY2002.

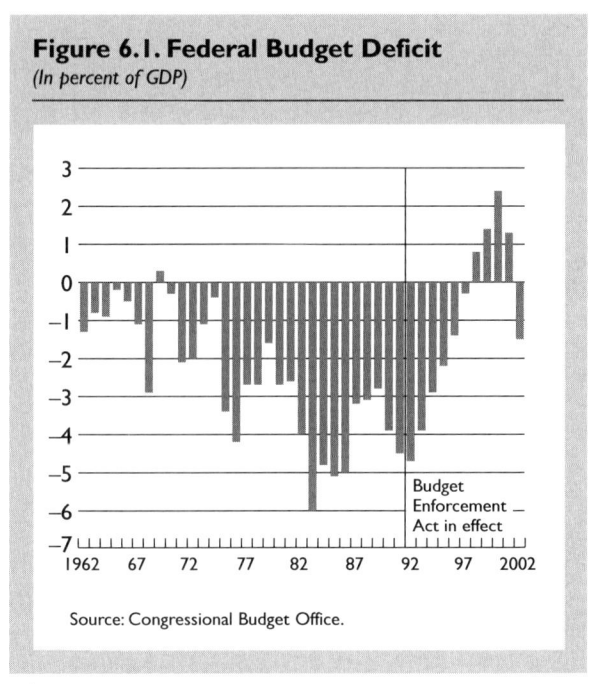

Figure 6.1. Federal Budget Deficit
(In percent of GDP)

Source: Congressional Budget Office.

---

[1]The fiscal year runs from October 1 to September 30.

Box 6.1. Main Provisions of the BEA

The BEA has three main features:

Caps on discretionary spending: Discretionary spending consists of outlays not covered by permanent law and represents roughly one-third of total federal outlays, including almost all defense expenditure, salaries and other operating expenses of government, and many grant programs. The BEA defines limits, or "caps," in nominal terms for specific discretionary spending categories for each fiscal year over a five-year period, with separate caps set for budget authority and actual outlays. At present, there is a cap for overall discretionary spending, as well as separate caps for highway, mass transit, and conservation spending, but at different times during the 1990s, either a single cap for all discretionary spending or separate caps for different spending categories have applied. The legislation allows for breaches of the caps in the case of "emergencies."

Pay-as-you-go (PAYGO): The PAYGO requirement covers tax receipts and mandatory, or direct, spending. Mandatory spending is controlled by permanent laws and includes Medicare, Medicaid, unemployment benefits, and farm price supports. Under PAYGO, any legislation that increases mandatory spending or reduces revenues must be accompanied by legislation that spec-

ifies offsetting mandatory spending reductions or tax increases over a five-year period. PAYGO rules do not apply to changes in mandatory spending and receipts that are not the result of new laws, such as the effects of cost-of-living increases, interest rate changes, or demographic changes. PAYGO does not apply to Social Security.

Sequestration: Sequestration procedures are used to enforce the BEA. For discretionary spending, if the amount of budget authority specified in an appropriation act, or the outlays in a particular year, exceed the corresponding caps, the BEA requires a reduction in spending in the relevant category by a uniform percentage. Special rules are specified for reducing some programs, and others are exempt from sequestration entirely. For mandatory spending and revenues, the Office of Management and Budget is required to estimate whether the new laws enacted meet the PAYGO requirements. If they do not, a uniform reduction is required across all mandatory spending programs that are not exempt or subject to special rules. These latter categories cover Social Security, interest on public debt, Medicaid, and Medicare, leaving only 3 percent of mandatory spending subject to sequestration. Sequestration procedures have been enacted only once—in 1991.

Assessing the BEA Rules

Deficit reduction during the 1990s reflected the effects of both buoyant tax revenues and expenditure restraint (Figure 6.2). It is impossible to say with certainty how much the BEA rules contributed to this fiscal consolidation, not least because the counterfactual—that is, what the deficit would have been in the absence of these rules—is not known. Nonetheless, the effectiveness of BEA rules is reviewed below from a variety of different perspectives: the design of the BEA's enforcement mechanism compared with those of GRH; trends in spending; accounting for the role of economic growth in reducing the deficit; and enforcement and budget transparency issues.

BEA Design Improvements

The BEA's enforcement mechanisms were widely viewed as a significant improvement over those in the GRH in at least three ways:[2]

- First, BEA rules applied to outturns, while GRH simply imposed constraints on deficit projec-

---
[2]See Reischauer (1997); Blinder and Yellen (2001); GAO (2002); and Penner (2002).

tions and thereby encouraged budgets to be based on overly optimistic macroeconomic assumptions.

- Second, the deficit targets under GRH were subject to many factors beyond government control, including fluctuations in mandatory spending. By contrast, the BEA caps applied to discretionary spending, over which the government has more direct control, while a pay-as-you-go provision required that legislated changes to mandatory spending programs or tax provisions had to be budget neutral over a 5-year (later 10-year) period, introducing greater accountability into the budget process.

- Third, under GRH, the combination of overoptimistic macroeconomic assumptions and nominal deficit targets rendered the amounts of budgetary funds subject to sequestration so large that the enforcement process lost credibility. Sequestration under the BEA, although only applied once in 1991, has been a more credible deterrent—at least until the late 1990s when it was circumvented by large emergency appropriations and adjustments to spending caps, as discussed below.

Figure 6.2. Federal Outlays and Revenues
(In percent of GDP)

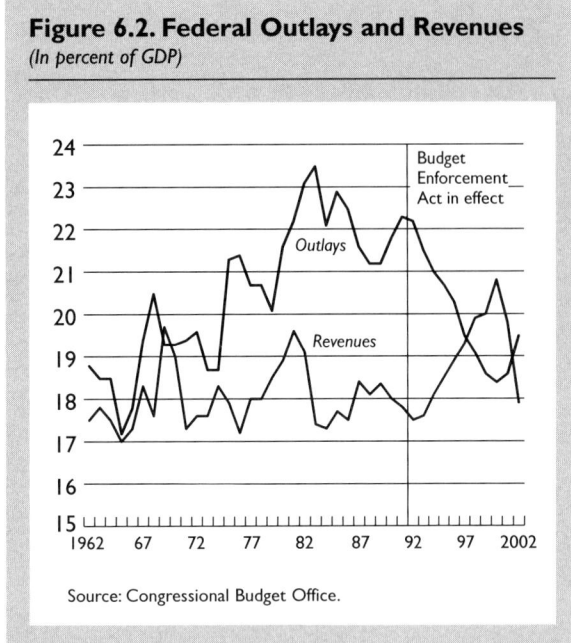

Source: Congressional Budget Office.

Assessing BEA's Effectiveness

Deficit reduction through most of the 1990s rested in part on a massive decline in defense expenditure following the end of the Cold War, and a leveling off in other discretionary outlays. During FY1991–FY1998, discretionary spending outlays remained within the BEA ceilings (with only minor adjustments to the original caps), and consequently declined relative to GDP (Table 6.1; Figure 6.3). Underlying this trend were substantial reductions in defense spending, which provided some room for nondefense spending to increase after separate defense and nondefense caps expired at the end of FY1993. From a longer-term perspective, however, nondefense discretionary spending increased steadily relative to GDP during the 1960s and 1970s, fell in the 1980s, and remained broadly constant during the 1990s. This suggests that BEA spending ceilings largely served to lock in spending reductions achieved in the 1980s rather than precipitating a major reduction in discretionary outlays.

The BEA also appears to have had a noticeable impact on mandatory spending. Mandatory spending fell slightly as a share of GDP between FY1991 and FY2002 (Figure 6.4). Although PAYGO did not completely halt the enactment of new spending initiatives—for example, the children's health insurance program was enacted in the late 1990s—several studies have argued that the PAYGO requirement was effective in discouraging new mandatory spending initiatives and tax cuts. Elmendorf, Liebman, and Wilcox (2001), for example, emphasized the relative *lack* of tax cuts and spending increases in the face of large surpluses at the end of the 1990s.[3] In addition, Schick (2000) argued that the PAYGO rules may

---

[3] See also Joyce (1996) and CBO (2002).

Table 6.1. Adjustments to Discretionary Spending Caps
(In billions of U.S. dollars)

	1991	1992	1993	1994	1995	1996	1997	1998	1999	2000	2001	2002
Statutory caps set in BEA[1]	514.4	524.9	534.0	534.8	540.8	547.3	547.3	547.9	559.3	564.3	564.4	560.8
Adjustments for changes in:												
Concepts/definitions		1.0	2.4	2.3	3.0	–0.5	–2.6	–2.8	–0.3	0.1	–0.1	–3.3
Inflation		–0.3	–2.5	–5.8	–8.8	1.8	2.3	0.9				
Emergency requirements	1.1	1.8	5.4	9.0	10.1	6.4	8.1	7.0	22.9	35.8	20.5	31.7
Desert Shield/Desert Storm	33.3	14.9	7.6	2.8	1.1	0.0						
Amendments for FY2001											58.6	
Amendments for FY2002												133.1
Revised spending limits[2]	551.6	545.7	550.4	547.6	548.7	552.7	553.6	560.2	584.2	604.2	652.2	731.3
Outlays[3]	533.3	533.8	539.4	541.4	544.9	532.7	547.2	552.1	572.0	614.8	657.4	740.5

Source: Office of Management and Budget.
[1] Budget Enforcement Act (BEA) as amended in 1993 and 1997.
[2] Numerous smaller adjustments not shown.
[3] 2002 figure is an estimate, as of January 2002.

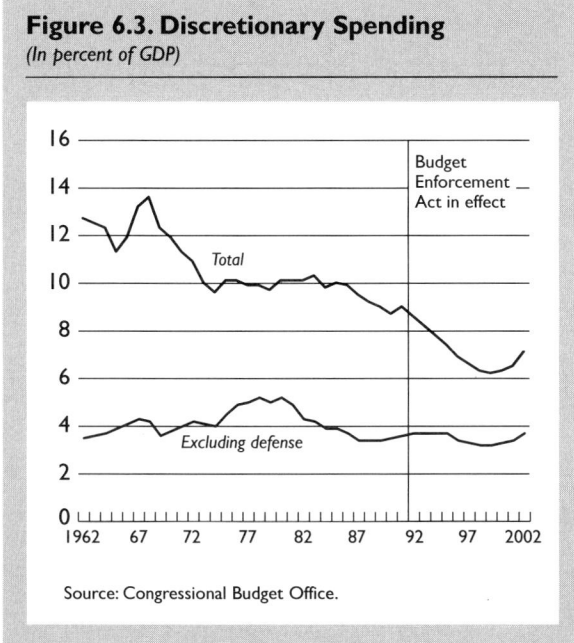

Figure 6.3. Discretionary Spending
(In percent of GDP)

Source: Congressional Budget Office.

have encouraged some reforms of the welfare system, such as converting Aid to Families with Dependent Children (AFDC) from an open-ended entitlement to a fixed block grant.

In achieving fiscal consolidation, however, the effectiveness of BEA rules was likely enhanced by the economic boom of the 1990s. Anderson (1999) notes that while discretionary spending outturns were close to the BEA limits between FY1993 and FY1998, outturns for mandatory spending and revenues were very different from the projections made in January 1993. He argues, therefore, that the effects of unexpectedly strong growth on revenues and mandatory spending were more important than the limits on discretionary spending in achieving deficit reduction. This is illustrated in Figure 6.5, which shows the rise in the Congressional Budget Office's one-year-ahead forecast error for revenues and expenditure that can be ascribed to economic factors in the late 1990s.

BEA Circumvention and Fiscal Complexity

Budget discipline eroded significantly with the emergence of actual and prospective budget surpluses beginning in FY1999. Spending caps and PAYGO, which had remained notionally in place, were routinely circumvented, and expenditure ceilings for 2001 and 2002 were adjusted upward in 1997 (see Table 6.1). As a result of this—as well as reflecting additional outlays enacted following the September 11 attacks—federal outlays as a share of

GDP increased by about ¾ percent between FY1999 and FY2002.

The devices used to circumvent BEA rules included the following:[4]

- Emergency appropriations were exempt from BEA rules, and the specific criteria for defining an emergency were not codified. This exemption was used infrequently between FY1991 and FY1998, when annual adjustments to the caps for emergency requirements averaged less than $7 billion. During FY1999 and FY2000, however, annual emergency appropriations increased to over $30 billion, including appropriations for the long-anticipated 2000 census and farm subsidies.

- Advance appropriations occur when Congress appropriates funds for spending in a future year. Although advance appropriations were to be counted toward spending caps in future years, they were increasingly used from FY1999, increasing pressure on subsequent budgets to either raise the ceilings or engage in other accounting mechanisms to augment spending.

- Budgetary measures could be structured in a way to reduce costs during the budget period that was subject to scoring. For example, extensions to Medicaid in the late 1980s and early 1990s were phased in such a way that the spending increase took place only after the current scoring period. Once the next year's expenditure baseline was established, the increase was already authorized by law. Alternatively, the 2001 tax cuts included a "sunset" provision to repeal all measures at the end of 2010, thereby reducing the cost of the measures during the FY2002–FY2011 budget window.

- An expiring tax could be extended repeatedly. For example, the federal tax on airline tickets expired in 1996 but was renewed in 1997 and 1998, allowing revenue gains to be scored as offsets to other measures. In contrast, a permanent tax increase could only be scored once.

- The CBO and the Office of Management and Budget (OMB) maintained a "scorecard" of the cumulative effect of legislated changes on the budget balance during a congressional year. Under normal application of the PAYGO rules, if the calculated net change was negative, then offsets had to be found. However, this requirement could be circumvented by setting the PAYGO scorecard to zero. For example, legisla-

---

[4]For further discussion, see Schick (2000).

tion enacted by the 107th Congress, including the June 2001 tax cuts, reduced the overall budget surplus, but offsetting actions were not required because Congress enacted other legislation that instructed OMB to change the PAYGO balances for 2001 and 2002 to zero.

The BEA's impact on budget transparency was also mixed. On the one hand, the above list suggests that the BEA encouraged using complex accounting devices to circumvent budget rules, and some analysts have also suggested that the BEA constraints may also have encouraged Congress to resort to extrabudgetary policy instruments, including regulations and unfunded mandates. Nonetheless, the BEA arguably improved fiscal transparency in many respects, including by requiring full listings, cost estimates, and intensified scrutiny of all tax expenditures. In addition, the scorekeeping guidelines were codified and published in the 1997 Balanced Budget Act. At the same time, the scorekeeping period was extended from 5 to 10 years, in an attempt to reduce the scope for timing shifts. Finally, several studies have concluded that the BEA has resulted in less gimmickry than occurred under GRH.[5]

Options for Reform

Given the recent erosion of the U.S. fiscal position and the longer-term fiscal pressures implied by demographic trends, there is an evident need for strengthening budget discipline. Both U.S. and international experience have amply demonstrated that fiscal rules cannot substitute for an underlying political commitment to fiscal discipline and longer-term fiscal sustainability, and the revenue and expenditure policies that would be required.[6] Nonetheless, the U.S. experience between 1990 and 1998 suggests that, with political commitment, BEA-type rules can play a useful role in bolstering budget discipline.

At the same time, however, the erosion of the effectiveness of BEA rules during the more recent period indicates the need for reform. Some of the specific options under discussion include the following:[7]

---

[5]See, for example, Auerbach (1994) and Joyce (1996).

[6]Hemming and Kell (2001).

[7]See GAO (2002) and other submissions to the House Committee on the Budget. The administration's FY2003 and FY2004 budgets also included some proposals that went beyond simply refining the caps and PAYGO provisions, such as replacing Congress's Concurrent Resolution with a Joint Budget Resolution, approved by the Congress and signed by the President, that would have the force of law; correcting the constitutional flaw in the Line Item Veto Act, and linking the caps to debt reduction; and introducing biennial budgeting. The FY2004 budget proposed to extend BEA's PAYGO provisions and caps on discretionary spending, which expired at the end of FY2002, for two years.

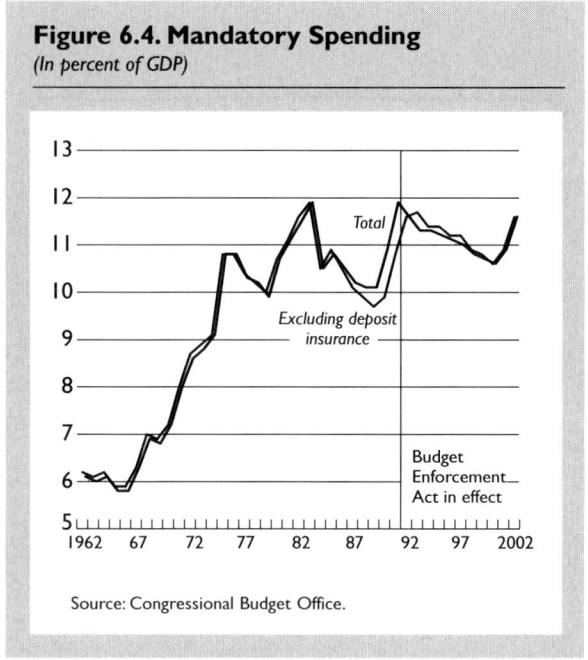

Figure 6.4. Mandatory Spending
(In percent of GDP)

Source: Congressional Budget Office.

- Limit discretionary spending caps to budget authority only. Some argue that separate caps on budget authority and outlays created incentives for delaying obligations and favored programs with slower spend-out rates. Focusing the caps simply on appropriations would also improve accountability, given that Congress has more control in a given year over budget appropriations as opposed to outlays.

- Clarify and codify into law the criteria for emergency spending. For example, the House Budget Resolution for FY2002 defined an emergency as a situation (other than a threat to national security) that requires new budget authority to prevent the imminent loss of life or property, and is sudden, urgent, unforeseen, and temporary. This more stringent definition could be combined with the introduction of a contingency reserve for emergencies, which would be included in the spending cap, possibly calculated as an average of emergency/disaster spending over the past 5 or 10 years.

- Redesign PAYGO to trigger examination of the "base." Under the current rules, cost increases of existing mandatory programs are exempt from the PAYGO requirement. This provision favors existing policies over possible new programs and constrains the budget from reflecting current priorities. Recent suggestions have included the introduction of "look back" procedures: Congress would specify targets for mandatory

Figure 6.5. Projection Errors Due to Economic Factors[1]
(In billions of U.S. dollars)

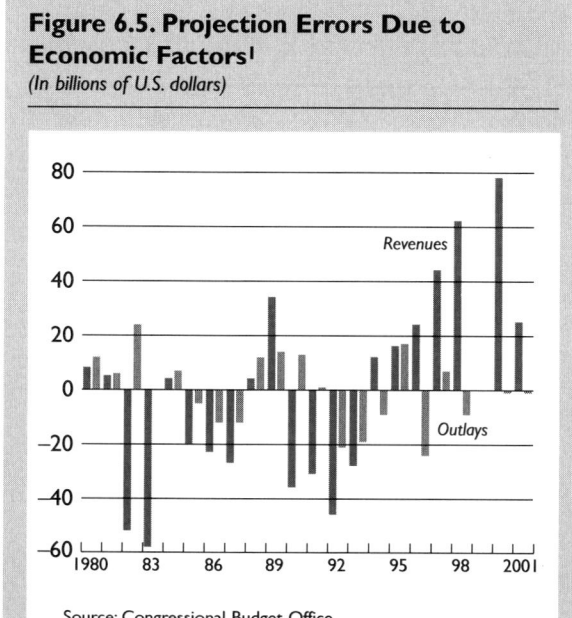

Source: Congressional Budget Office.
[1]No data available for 1999.

programs several years into the future; if these targets are or seem likely to be exceeded, the President could recommend in his budget that some or all of the average be recouped.

- Make the PAYGO requirement contingent on a level or forecast of the debt-to-GDP ratio. Under this approach, additional spending or tax cuts would be permitted without offsetting measures if the debt ratio is below some key level, or projected to decline by a certain amount. This would help prevent PAYGO from becoming overly restrictive if fiscal outturns are better than expected.

- Clarify and refine the scorekeeping guidelines. One option would be to require all tax and spending programs to be scored as fully phased in within, say, five years, preventing the use of a gradual phasing of measures to reduce their scorecard cost below the true long-term cost. A second possibility would be to codify criteria for deciding which receipts are classified as revenue, and are therefore subject to PAYGO requirements, and which ones as user fees that can be used to offset discretionary spending.

Conclusion

As discussed in Section I, impending demographic and other pressures on the federal budget make it increasingly urgent to establish a framework for achieving long-term fiscal sustainability. The U.S. experience of the 1990s under the Budget Enforcement Act, and the international experience with fiscal responsibility legislations, illustrate that budget rules, if properly defined, can help discipline policies and provide the appropriate context for weighing tax and expenditure policy options. Reintroducing strengthened versions of the BEA's budget rules could help provide the necessary framework for achieving the fiscal adjustment that is needed in the period ahead, especially if it is accompanied by a strong underlying political commitment to fiscal discipline and balanced budgets.

References

Anderson, B., 1999, "Budgeting in a Surplus Environment," paper prepared for the 1999 Annual Meeting of Senior Budget Officials (Paris: OECD).

Auerbach, A.J., 1994, "The U.S. Fiscal Problem: Where We Are, How We Got Here and Where We Are Going," in *NBER Macroeconomics Manual*, Vol. 9, edited by S. Fischer and J. Rotemberg (Cambridge, Massachusetts: MIT Press).

Blinder, A., and J. Yellen, 2001, *The Fabulous Decade: Macroeconomic Lessons from the 1990s* (Washington: Century Foundation Press).

Congressional Budget Office (CBO), 2002, *Budget and Economic Outlook, Fiscal Years 2003–12* (Washington: U.S. Government Printing Office).

Elmendorf, D., J. Liebman, and D. Wilcox, 2001, "Fiscal Policy and Social Security Policy During the 1990s," NBER Working Paper No. 8488 (Cambridge, Massachusetts: National Bureau of Economic Research).

General Accounting Office (GAO), 2002, "Budget Process: Extending Budget Controls," Testimony Before the Committee on the Budget, Washington, April 25.

Hemming, R., and M. Kell, 2001, "Promoting Fiscal Responsibility: Transparency, Rules, and Independent Fiscal Authorities," paper presented at the Bank of Italy Fiscal Rules Workshop, Perugia, 2001.

Joyce, P., 1996, "Congressional Budget Reform: The Unanticipated Implications for Federal Policy Making," *Public Administration Review*, Vol. 56, No. 4, pp. 317–24.

Penner, R., 2002, "Repairing the Congressional Budget Process," *Research Report* (Washington: Urban Institute). Available via Internet: www.urban.org.

Reischauer, R., 1997, "The Unfulfillable Promise," in *Setting National Priorities: Budget Choices for the Next Century,* edited by R. Reischauer (Washington: Brookings Institution).

Schick, A., and F. Lostracco, 2000, *The Federal Budget: Politics, Policy, Process,* rev. ed. (Washington: Brookings Institution).

VII Will the State and Local Budget Crisis Hinder Economic Growth?

Iryna Ivaschenko

Following a decade of strong revenue growth and significant surpluses, state and local governments (SLGs) are now facing significant budget shortfalls for a third consecutive year. At a time when the federal government has embarked on expansionary fiscal policies to support economic activity, these shortfalls have raised concerns that corrective budgetary measures taken by SLGs could counteract federal government stimulus and dampen economic activity. This chapter reviews the principal causes of the state and local fiscal crisis and attempts to quantify its macroeconomic implications.

State and Local Government Finances

The SLG sector represents an important and growing part of the overall economy. Current expendi-

tures—that is, total spending excluding outlays on capital investments—by SLGs have grown strongly in recent decades, accounting for nearly all of the 7 percent of GDP increase in general government spending since 1960 (Table 7.1).[1] Moreover, SLG investment has remained essentially constant in relation to GDP over time, which, given the decline in federal investment, has also made SLGs the principal source of public investment. Growing SLG expenditures have been financed by tax and other revenue increases, amounting to 4½ percent of GDP since 1960, as well as an increase in federal grants of 2 percent of GDP. Indeed, federal grants have become

---

[1]State and local governments are typically aggregated because the breakdown of data between these two levels of government varies across states (see Stotsky and Sunley, 1997, and references therein). Local government expenditures were of roughly the same magnitude as those of state governments during 1960–90.

Table 7.1. Government Revenues, Spending, and Investment
(In percent of GDP)

	1960	1980	1990	2002
Current receipts				
General government[1]	24.9	27.4	27.7	27.5
Federal government	17.6	18.7	18.2	17.9
State and local governments	8.0	11.3	11.4	12.5
Federal grants-in-aid to state and local governments	0.8	2.6	1.9	2.9
Current expenditures				
General government[1]	22.7	29.0	30.6	29.9
Federal government	16.3	20.6	21.2	19.9
Federal grants-in-aid to state and local governments	0.8	2.6	1.9	2.9
State and local governments	7.2	11.0	11.4	13.0
Gross investment				
General government	5.4	3.6	3.7	3.4
Federal government	2.7	1.3	1.5	1.0
State and local governments	2.6	2.3	2.2	2.3

Source: National Income and Product Accounts.
[1]Excluding intergovernmental transfers.

Table 7.2. State and Local Governments: Composition of Receipts
(In percent of total receipts)

	1960	1980	1990	2002
Personal income tax receipts	6.0	13.4	16.2	15.4
Corporate profits tax accruals	3.0	4.6	3.4	2.6
Sales taxes	28.7	26.2	27.6	25.6
Property taxes	38.4	21.7	24.3	20.5
Contributions for social insurance	1.1	1.1	1.5	0.7
Federal grants-in-aid	9.5	22.8	16.8	23.4

Source: National Income and Product Accounts.

significantly more important for SLGs, accounting for almost one-fourth of total revenues in 2002 (Table 7.2).

The strong increase in SLG spending and federal grant receipts reflects, in part, a response to growing expenditure mandates imposed by the federal government. In the United States, SLGs are the primary provider of government services such as education, public infrastructure, and public health and safety. However, a substantial proportion of SLG spending in these areas is funded by grants, loans, and tax subsidies from the federal government, which are used to buttress federal mandates that specify the level of services to be provided by the states, including for welfare, Medicaid, and education programs.[2] For example, states participating in Medicaid must adhere to the requirements of the Medicaid Act, which specifies and defines categories of medical services for which federal reimbursement is allowed, and requires that states cover mandatory categories (O'Connell, Watson, and Butler, 2003). Over half of federal transfers have been directed toward such programs, which has contributed to a growing proportion of state expenditure also being channeled in these areas.

On the tax side, however, there is little coordination of federal and state policies, with the result that states differ greatly in how revenues are raised. The Constitution grants federal and state governments independent taxing powers, and local governments derive their taxing powers from state governments. As a result, each level of government imposes and administers its taxes independently, and there are no tax-sharing arrangements between the federal and state governments (Stotsky and Sunley, 1997).[3] However, states typically piggyback on the federal income tax code by using federal definitions of personal and corporate taxable income before applying state-specific adjustments. For corporate taxes, most states also use the depreciation schedule applied by the federal government. Nonetheless, the degree of conformity between federal and state tax systems differs significantly across states.

Recent Developments in State and Local Government Finances

The economic slowdown in recent years has contributed to a significant deterioration in the fiscal position of state and local governments. At the end of the 1990s, SLGs were running current surpluses—that is, excluding spending on capital investments—of up to around ½ percent of GDP, largely reflecting the benefits of solid economic growth (Figure 7.1). As the economy slowed, however, state and local governments fell back into deficit in late 2000, with current deficits reaching a post–World War II peak of ½ percent of GDP in 2002. The budgetary situation among the states remains difficult—with almost 90 percent of states projecting revenue shortfalls that will exceed 5 percent of their general funds, their deficit could reach ½ percent of GDP in FY2004.[4]

---

[2]Federal grants for Medicaid are currently administered on a cost-sharing basis, with the federal share varying across states—from 50 to 80 percent—depending on the state's per capita income. Welfare programs are financed on a block-grant basis.

[3]Historically, state estate taxes have been set equal to or above the federal estate tax credit—a credit that taxpayers receive against their federal estate tax liability for state estate and inheritance tax payments. However, the federal estate tax is scheduled for repeal beginning in 2005 under the administration's 2001 tax package. State and local income taxes and property taxes are deductible from federally taxable income.

[4]In most states, the fiscal year runs from July 1 to June 30. The budgetary forecast for FY2004 is based on data provided to the National Conference of State Legislatures; and from NGA and NASBO (2003).

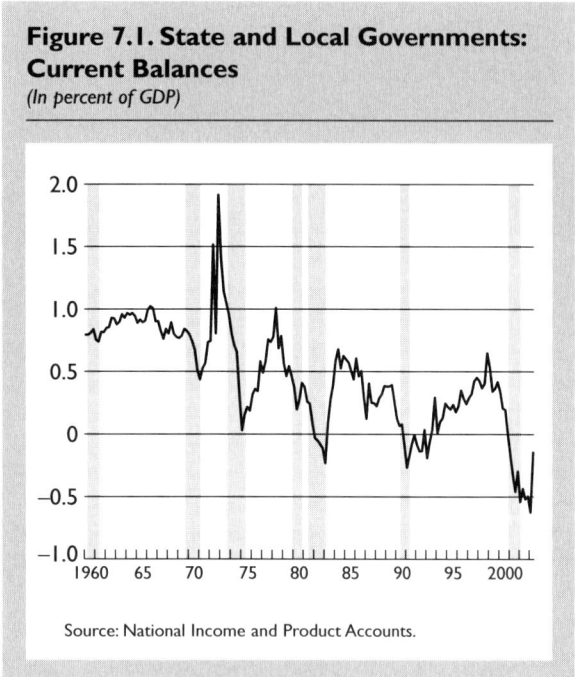

Figure 7.1. State and Local Governments: Current Balances
(In percent of GDP)

Source: National Income and Product Accounts.

The erosion in the fiscal position of the states appears largely to have reflected sharp increases in spending (Figure 7.2a). Most notably, outlays on health-related programs increased by ½ percent of GDP from the late 1990s, largely driven by the Medicaid program (Figure 7.2b, Table 7.3). The demands on the Medicaid system—which provides services to the poor—increased partly as a result of the recession, but many states had become more generous during the 1990s, and broader pressures on U.S. health care costs also played a major role (NASBO and NGA, 2003). The economic downturn and the associated increase in unemployment also boosted SLG spending on income-support and welfare programs after 1999.

At the same time, a sharp drop in income tax collections hurt states on the revenue side. Corporate and personal income tax revenues represent roughly one-fifth of total state receipts, and both these revenue sources declined by roughly ¼ percent of GDP during 2001 and 2002 (see Table 7.2). Other revenue sources, including sales and property taxes, remained relatively robust, reflecting the strength of consumer demand and the housing market.

Several factors have contributed to the sharp decline in income tax revenues:

- The economic slowdown dampened labor incomes, and the collapse of the stock market severely eroded capital gains, especially in California and on the East Coast, where a consider-

able amount of personal wealth is concentrated (Figure 7.2c).

- States had responded to the revenue boom of the late 1990s by cutting tax rates, including on property, which left them more dependent on cyclically sensitive revenue sources such as income tax (Figure 7.2d).[5]

- Tax cuts at the federal level have also had a (relatively modest) effect on SLG revenues—the 2001 and 2003 tax cuts are estimated to lower state tax revenues by about $5 billion.[6]

Balanced Budget Rules and Fiscal Adjustment

All states but one are required—either by state constitution or state law—to maintain a balanced budget.[7] However, there are several reasons why these requirements have not typically imposed a hard fiscal constraint in the past. Balanced budget laws typically apply only to current budgets, and states are permitted to borrow to fund capital spending. Moreover, there is often some scope to circumvent balanced budget constraints on a temporary basis. For example, many states are only required to balance their budgets on an ex ante basis, and most states have scope to delay payments and shift spending into future years by building arrears (NASBO, 2002). In addition, until recently, states have been able to draw on significant reserve funds accumulated during the surplus years of the 1990s.

The depletion of reserve funds means, however, that more difficult adjustments lie ahead. By the end of FY2000, state reserve funds had risen to around 10 percent of state expenditures from less than 5 percent at the end of the 1980s. However, in recent years, some 16 states have had to cover their deficits by drawing down these reserves, leaving overall reserve balances virtually exhausted by end-FY2003. This sharp turnaround has led some com-

---

[5]Johnson (2002) estimates ongoing revenue losses from tax cuts at around $40 billion. See also Rivlin (2003).

[6]Specifically, the following measures in the Economic Growth and Tax Relief Reconciliation Act of 2001 affected states' taxable income base: the increased standard deduction, new rules for individual retirement accounts, and additional deductions for education expenses. In addition, the recently enacted Jobs and Growth Tax Relief Reconciliation Act of 2003 is likely to further reduce state tax revenues. The "bonus depreciation" tax break for corporations, additional deductions for small and midsize businesses, and increases in deduction for married couples are estimated to cost states $3 billion in lost revenues, absent any measures by states to undo the effect (Johnson, 2003; McLaughlin, 2002).

[7]Vermont does not have balanced budget restrictions of any form.

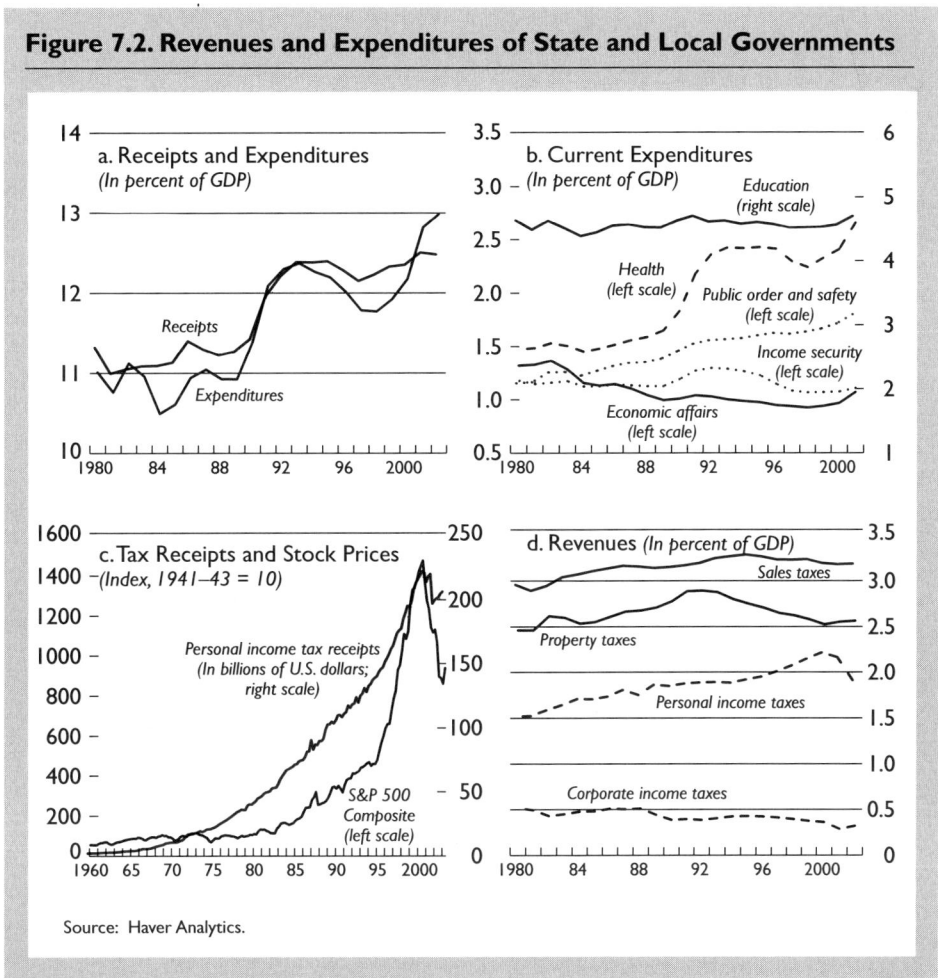

Figure 7.2. Revenues and Expenditures of State and Local Governments

a. Receipts and Expenditures
(In percent of GDP)

Receipts

Expenditures

b. Current Expenditures
(In percent of GDP)

Education
(right scale)

Health
(left scale)

Public order and safety
(left scale)

Income security
(left scale)

Economic affairs
(left scale)

c. Tax Receipts and Stock Prices
(Index, 1941–43 = 10)

Personal income tax receipts
(In billions of U.S. dollars;
right scale)

S&P 500
Composite
(left scale)

d. Revenues (In percent of GDP)

Sales taxes

Property taxes

Personal income taxes

Corporate income taxes

Source: Haver Analytics.

mentators to argue for easing legislative limits on the size of rainy day funds; some studies estimate that states would need reserves of more than 18 percent of expenditures to accommodate a macroeconomic shock of the magnitude of the 1990–91 recession (Lav and Berube, 1999).

States have already made substantial adjustments to control budget deficits in FY2002 and FY2003. On the spending side, measures have included hiring freezes, cuts in spending for prisons, education, child care, and support for local governments (NASBO and NGA, 2003). Medicaid spending has been largely excluded from cuts because of cost-sharing arrangements with the federal government, but states tightened eligibility requirements for optional participants and adopted cost-saving measures.[8] There has been considerable political resistance to tax hikes,

but states have made increased use of tobacco settlement funds, which amounted to $32 billion between 1998 and 2002 (Lindblom, 2003), to cover revenue shortfalls.

Nevertheless, states have been forced to increase their borrowing, possibly reflecting a reclassification of operating expenses as capital expenditures.[9] Outstanding market debt owed by state and local governments increased from 12 percent of GDP in 2000 to 14 percent in mid-2003, but still well below the 18 percent peak during the 1990–1991 recession (Figure 7.3). State credit ratings and risk premiums have not been significantly affected so far, except for several states that are facing more severe financial difficulties (Figure 7.4).[10]

---

[8]These included tightening eligibility requirements and creating preferred drug lists. Currently 19 states have authorized the use of such lists, compared with three states two years ago, according to the National Conference of State Legislatures. Drug expenses are one of the largest Medicaid spending items (*New York Times*, 2003).

[9]State and local governments can borrow to ease short-term revenue shortfalls. Stotsky and Sunley (1997) also note that some state governments used short-term borrowing to conceal deficits in their operating budgets.

[10]Premiums have widened for California, New York State, and New York City (*Financial Times*, 2003).

Table 7.3. State and Local Governments: Composition of Spending and Investment, 2002

(In percent)

	Spending	Investment
General public service	9.6	9.3
Public order and safety	14.1	4.6
Economic affairs	8.3	37.7
Housing and community services	0.6	8.9
Health	20.7	4.7
Education	36.7	31.6
Income security	8.6	0.7
Other	1.5	2.6
Total	100.0	100.0

Source: National Income and Product Accounts.

Budget difficulties are expected to worsen in FY2004. Surveys by the National Governors Association suggest that more cuts in program expenditures, including education, health services, and aid to local governments, are likely to take place. As a result, state spending is expected to fall by around ¼ percent in real terms in FY2004. In addition, governors in 29 states have recommended tax and fee increases for FY2004 with an expected yield of $17.5 billion (or 0.2 percent of GDP)—the largest since 1979.

How Much of a Drag on Growth?

The prospect of significant budgetary adjustments by SLGs raises questions about the possible effects on the broader macroeconomy and the recovery. The policy response by SLGs is likely to be procyclical and work against the substantial stimulus that has been injected by the fiscal and monetary authorities at the federal level.

Such concerns are partly alleviated by the fact that the size of budget shortfalls is relatively modest. For example, the analysis of changes in structural balances of the general and federal governments indicates that the adjustment by SLGs necessary to satisfy their balanced budget requirements would result in a fiscal contraction of about ¼ percent of GDP in 2003, offsetting only a small part of the fiscal stimulus injected at the federal level (Table 7.4).

Significant uncertainty surrounds estimates of the impact of fiscal policy on output. Most estimates for the United States place fiscal multipliers in the range of 0.3–1.4 for spending increases and 0.2–1.3 for tax cuts (Hemming, Kell, and Mahfouz, 2002).[11] The low end of these ranges are consistent with the view that the demand-side effects of expansionary fiscal policy are offset by Ricardian effects—that is, private saving rises in response to fiscal expansions as households prepare for higher future taxes. Indeed,

---

[11]Most of these results were obtained for the general government.

Figure 7.3. State and Local Governments: Credit Market Debt

(In percent of GDP)

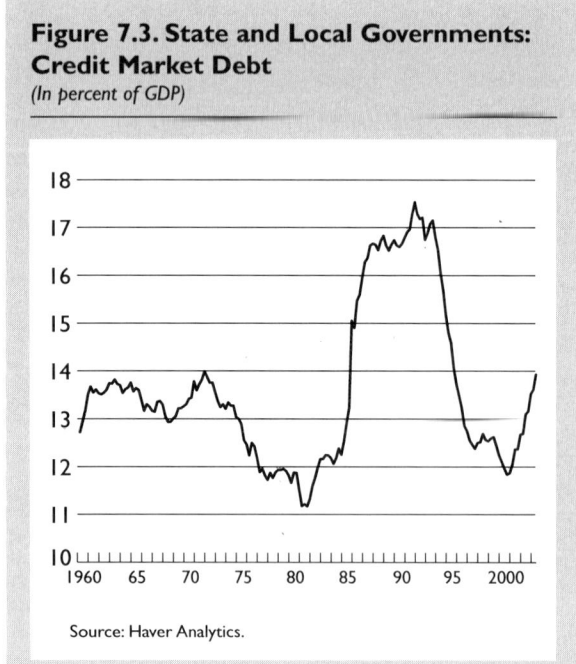

Source: Haver Analytics.

Figure 7.4. State and Local Governments: Budget Balances and Spreads on SLG Debt

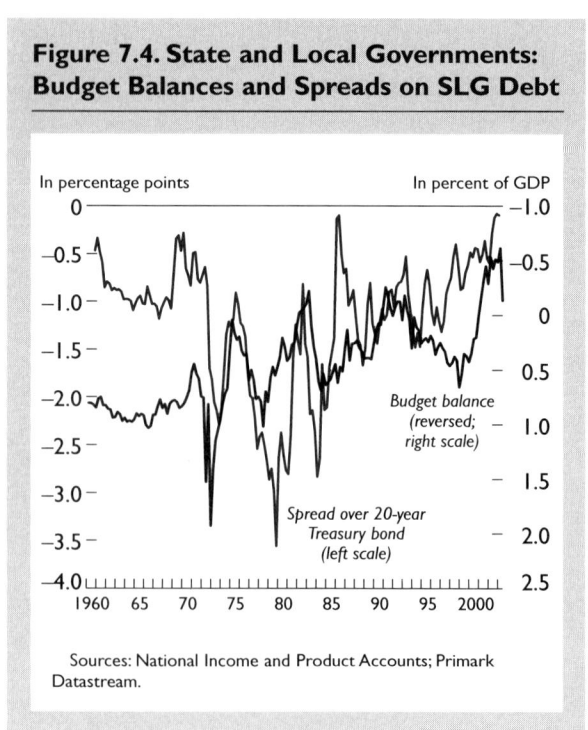

Sources: National Income and Product Accounts; Primark Datastream.

Table 7.4. Fiscal Impulse by Level of Government
(Calendar year data; in percent of GDP)

	2000	2001	2002	2003
Change in Actual Balances (NIPA basis)				
General government	0.7	−1.9	−3.0	−1.8
Federal government	0.5	−1.6	−2.7	−1.9
Change in Structural Balances				
General government	0.5	−1.1	−2.7	−1.5
Federal government				
(budget basis)	0.5	−1.2	−2.4	−1.7

Sources: *Budget of the U.S. Government*, various issues; and IMF staff estimates.

Figure 7.5. Dynamic Responses of the Output Gap to Fiscal Variables
(Dotted lines indicate two standard deviation range)

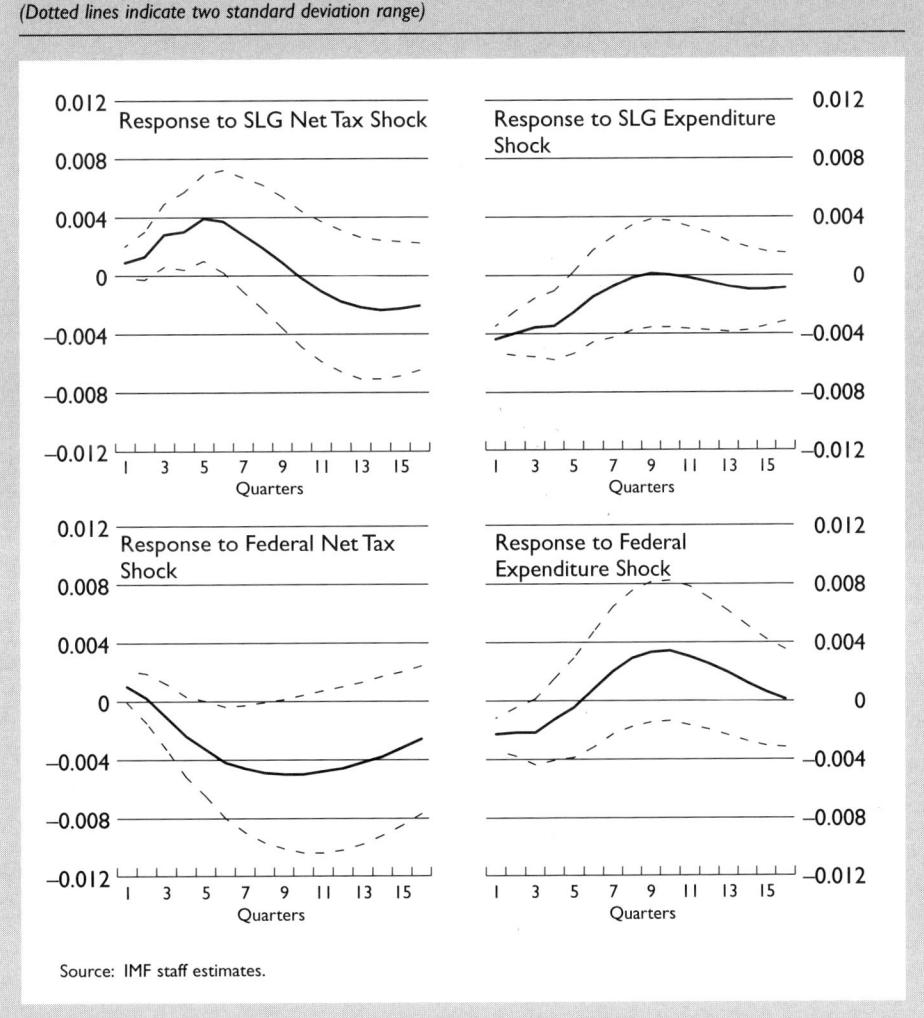

Source: IMF staff estimates.

some studies have suggested that fiscal multipliers can turn negative if fiscal policy increases uncertainty or is expected to crowd out private investment (Caballero and Pyndick, 1996; Krugman and Obstfeld, 1997).

The uncertainty that surrounds these multipliers is illustrated by the results of a simple vector-autoregression (VAR) model. The VAR approach allows for feedback among macroeconomic and fiscal variables, and has been used in a number of studies to assess the effects of monetary and fiscal policies on output (e.g., Blanchard and Perotti, 2002). The model employed in this study uses quarterly data on the output gap and both federal and SLG fiscal variables, so as to take into account feedbacks between policies at both levels of government. The specific fiscal variables were tax revenues net of transfers to persons; public consumption expenditure; and federal grants to SLGs. Fiscal variables were expressed as a ratio to GDP and detrended, using an HP filter to exclude long-term trends in the fiscal variables. Revenues and expenditures were also adjusted to exclude intergovernmental transfers. Four lags were employed in the VAR estimation, as suggested by several information criteria tests.

The results indicate that SLG spending and tax policies could have a significant temporary impact on real GDP. A one standard deviation shock to the share of SLG consumption spending in GDP would reduce the output gap—hence increase GDP—by 0.4 percentage points immediately, with the effect slowly decreasing to almost zero by the fifth quarter.[12] At the same time, a similar one standard deviation shock to SLG net taxes would have a negligible effect on GDP in the first quarter, with the impact slowly building and reaching almost 0.4 percentage points in the fifth quarter. The effect of the tax shock dissipates completely after six quarters (Figure 7.5).[13]

The results also indicate that fiscal policies of SLG have stronger impact on real GDP than the federal government. For example, a 1 percentage point increase in net federal taxes as a share of GDP would have no significant impact on the output gap, while a similar increase in federal spending would reduce the output gap by about 0.2 percentage points in the first quarter. However, the latter effect would entirely dissipate after three quarters.

---

[12]Generalized impulses—a modification of the Cholesky factorization that does not depend on the VAR ordering—are used in the estimation. See Pesaran and Shin (1998) for details.

[13]The estimation results should be interpreted with caution since most components of SLG budget data available in the National Income and Product Accounts (NIPA) are available only with a two-year lag and the most recent data are estimated. In addition, most quarterly data are being interpolated from the annual data.

References

Blanchard, O., and R. Perotti, 2002, "An Empirical Characterization of the Dynamic Effects of Changes in Government Spending and Taxes on Output," *Quarterly Journal of Economics*, Vol. 117, No. 4, pp. 1329–68.

Caballero, R., and P. Pyndick, 1996, "Uncertainty, Investment, and Industry Evolution," *International Economic Review*, Vol. 37, No. 3, pp. 641–62.

Financial Times, 2003, "U.S. States Borrow More to Ease Financial Crunch" (London), May 12.

Hemming, R., M. Kell, and S. Mahfouz, 2002, "The Effectiveness of Fiscal Policy in Stimulating Economic Activity—A Review of Literature," IMF Working Paper 02/208 (Washington: International Monetary Fund).

Johnson, N., 2002, "The State Tax Cuts of the 1990s, the Current Revenue Crisis, and Implications for State Service" (unpublished; Washington: Center on Budget and Policy Priorities).

————, 2003, "Federal Tax Changes Likely to Cost States Billions of Dollars in Coming Years" (unpublished; Washington: Center on Budget and Policy Priorities).

Krugman, P., and M. Obstfeld, 1997, *International Economics: Theory and Policy*, 4th ed. (Reading, Massachusetts: Addison-Wesley).

Lav, I., and A. Berube, 1999, "When It Rains, It Pours: A Look at the Adequacy of States' Rainy Day Funds and Budget Reserves" (unpublished; Washington: Center on Budget and Policy Priorities).

Lindblom, E., 2003, "Actual Payments Received by the States from the Tobacco Settlements," Fact Sheet (Washington: National Center for Tobacco-Free Kids) January 15.

McLaughlin, A., 2002, "Recent Federal Tax Legislation and the States" (Washington: National Conference of State Legislatures), July. Available via Internet: www.ncsl.org/statefed/taxconformity02.pdf.

National Association of State Budget Officers (NASBO), 2002, *Budget Processes in the States* (Washington: NASBO), January.

National Governors Association (NGA) and NASBO, 2003, *The Fiscal Survey of States* (Washington: NGA), June.

New York Times, 2003, "22 States Limiting Doctors' Latitude in Medicaid Drug," June 16.

O'Connell, M., S. Watson, and B. Butler, 2003, *Introduction to Medicaid: Eligibility, Federal Mandates, Hearings and Litigation* (Austin, Texas: Southern Disability Law Center). Available via Internet: www.nls.org/conf2003/medicaid-intro.htm.

Pesaran, H., and Y. Shin, 1998, "Generalized Impulse Response Analysis in Linear Multivariate Models," *Economic Letters*, Vol. 58, No. 1, pp. 17–29.

Rivlin, A., 2003, "Another State Fiscal Crisis: Is There a Better Way?" Welfare Reforms and Beyond, Policy Brief No. 23 (Washington: Brookings Institution).

Stotsky, J., and E. Sunley, 1997, "United States," in *Fiscal Federalism in Theory and Practice*, edited by Teresa Ter-Minassian (Washington: International Monetary Fund).

Recent Occasional Papers of the International Monetary Fund

227. U.S. Fiscal Policies and Priorities for Long-Run Sustainability, edited by Martin Mühleisen and Christopher Towe. 2004.

226. Hong Kong SAR: Meeting the Challenges of Integration with the Mainland, edited by Eswar Prasad, with contributions from Jorge Chan-Lau, Dora Iakova, William Lee, Hong Liang, Ida Liu, Papa N'Diaye, and Tao Wang. 2004.

225. Rules-Based Fiscal Policy in France, Germany, Italy, and Spain, by Teresa Dabán, Enrica Detragiache, Gabriel di Bella, Gian Maria Milesi-Ferretti, and Steven Symansky. 2003.

224. Managing Systemic Banking Crises, by a staff team led by David S. Hoelscher and Marc Quintyn. 2003.

223. Monetary Union Among Member Countries of the Gulf Cooperation Council, by a staff team led by Ugo Fasano. 2003.

222. Informal Funds Transfer Systems: An Analysis of the Informal Hawala System, by Mohammed El Qorchi, Samuel Munzele Maimbo, and John F. Wilson. 2003.

221. Deflation: Determinants, Risks, and Policy Options, by Manmohan S. Kumar. 2003.

220. Effects of Financial Globalization on Developing Countries: Some Empirical Evidence, by Eswar S. Prasad, Kenneth Rogoff, Shang-Jin Wei, and Ayhan Kose. 2003.

219. Economic Policy in a Highly Dollarized Economy: The Case of Cambodia, by Mario de Zamaroczy and Sopanha Sa. 2003.

218. Fiscal Vulnerability and Financial Crises in Emerging Market Economies, by Richard Hemming, Michael Kell, and Axel Schimmelpfennig. 2003.

217. Managing Financial Crises: Recent Experience and Lessons for Latin America, edited by Charles Collyns and G. Russell Kincaid. 2003.

216. Is the PRGF Living Up to Expectations?—An Assessment of Program Design, by Sanjeev Gupta, Mark Plant, Benedict Clements, Thomas Dorsey, Emanuele Baldacci, Gabriela Inchauste, Shamsuddin Tareq, and Nita Thacker. 2002.

215. Improving Large Taxpayers' Compliance: A Review of Country Experience, by Katherine Baer. 2002.

214. Advanced Country Experiences with Capital Account Liberalization, by Age Bakker and Bryan Chapple. 2002.

213. The Baltic Countries: Medium-Term Fiscal Issues Related to EU and NATO Accession, by Johannes Mueller, Christian Beddies, Robert Burgess, Vitali Kramarenko, and Joannes Mongardini. 2002.

212. Financial Soundness Indicators: Analytical Aspects and Country Practices, by V. Sundararajan, Charles Enoch, Armida San José, Paul Hilbers, Russell Krueger, Marina Moretti, and Graham Slack. 2002.

211. Capital Account Liberalization and Financial Sector Stability, by a staff team led by Shogo Ishii and Karl Habermeier. 2002.

210. IMF-Supported Programs in Capital Account Crises, by Atish Ghosh, Timothy Lane, Marianne Schulze-Ghattas, Alesv Bulírv, Javier Hamann, and Alex Mourmouras. 2002.

209. Methodology for Current Account and Exchange Rate Assessments, by Peter Isard, Hamid Faruqee, G. Russell Kincaid, and Martin Fetherston. 2001.

208. Yemen in the 1990s: From Unification to Economic Reform, by Klaus Enders, Sherwyn Williams, Nada Choueiri, Yuri Sobolev, and Jan Walliser. 2001.

207. Malaysia: From Crisis to Recovery, by Kanitta Meesook, Il Houng Lee, Olin Liu, Yougesh Khatri, Natalia Tamirisa, Michael Moore, and Mark H. Krysl. 2001.

206. The Dominican Republic: Stabilization, Structural Reform, and Economic Growth, by a staff team led by Philip Young, comprising Alessandro Giustiniani, Werner C. Keller, Randa E. Sab, and others. 2001.

205. Stabilization and Savings Funds for Nonrenewable Resources, by Jeffrey Davis, Rolando Ossowski, James Daniel, and Steven Barnett. 2001.

204. Monetary Union in West Africa (ECOWAS): Is It Desirable and How Could It Be Achieved? by Paul Masson and Catherine Pattillo. 2001.

203. Modern Banking and OTC Derivatives Markets: The Transformation of Global Finance and Its Implications for Systemic Risk, by Garry J. Schinasi, R. Sean Craig, Burkhard Drees, and Charles Kramer. 2000.

202. Adopting Inflation Targeting: Practical Issues for Emerging Market Countries, by Andrea Schaechter, Mark R. Stone, and Mark Zelmer. 2000.

201. Developments and Challenges in the Caribbean Region, by Samuel Itam, Simon Cueva, Erik Lundback, Janet Stotsky, and Stephen Tokarick. 2000.

200. Pension Reform in the Baltics: Issues and Prospects, by Jerald Schiff, Niko Hobdari, Axel Schimmelpfennig, and Roman Zytek. 2000.

199. Ghana: Economic Development in a Democratic Environment, by Sérgio Pereira Leite, Anthony Pellechio, Luisa Zanforlin, Girma Begashaw, Stefania Fabrizio, and Joachim Harnack. 2000.

198. Setting Up Treasuries in the Baltics, Russia, and Other Countries of the Former Soviet Union: An Assessment of IMF Technical Assistance, by Barry H. Potter and Jack Diamond. 2000.

197. Deposit Insurance: Actual and Good Practices, by Gillian G.H. Garcia. 2000.

196. Trade and Trade Policies in Eastern and Southern Africa, by a staff team led by Arvind Subramanian, with Enrique Gelbard, Richard Harmsen, Katrin Elborgh-Woytek, and Piroska Nagy. 2000.

195. The Eastern Caribbean Currency Union—Institutions, Performance, and Policy Issues, by Frits van Beek, José Roberto Rosales, Mayra Zermeño, Ruby Randall, and Jorge Shepherd. 2000.

194. Fiscal and Macroeconomic Impact of Privatization, by Jeffrey Davis, Rolando Ossowski, Thomas Richardson, and Steven Barnett. 2000.

193. Exchange Rate Regimes in an Increasingly Integrated World Economy, by Michael Mussa, Paul Masson, Alexander Swoboda, Esteban Jadresic, Paolo Mauro, and Andy Berg. 2000.

192. Macroprudential Indicators of Financial System Soundness, by a staff team led by Owen Evans, Alfredo M. Leone, Mahinder Gill, and Paul Hilbers. 2000.

191. Social Issues in IMF-Supported Programs, by Sanjeev Gupta, Louis Dicks-Mireaux, Ritha Khemani, Calvin McDonald, and Marijn Verhoeven. 2000.

190. Capital Controls: Country Experiences with Their Use and Liberalization, by Akira Ariyoshi, Karl Habermeier, Bernard Laurens, Inci Ötker-Robe, Jorge Iván Canales Kriljenko, and Andrei Kirilenko. 2000.

189. Current Account and External Sustainability in the Baltics, Russia, and Other Countries of the Former Soviet Union, by Donal McGettigan. 2000.

188. Financial Sector Crisis and Restructuring: Lessons from Asia, by Carl-Johan Lindgren, Tomás J.T. Baliño, Charles Enoch, Anne-Marie Gulde, Marc Quintyn, and Leslie Teo. 1999.

187. Philippines: Toward Sustainable and Rapid Growth, Recent Developments and the Agenda Ahead, by Markus Rodlauer, Prakash Loungani, Vivek Arora, Charalambos Christofides, Enrique G. De la Piedra, Piyabha Kongsamut, Kristina Kostial, Victoria Summers, and Athanasios Vamvakidis. 2000.

186. Anticipating Balance of Payments Crises: The Role of Early Warning Systems, by Andrew Berg, Eduardo Borensztein, Gian Maria Milesi-Ferretti, and Catherine Pattillo. 1999.

185. Oman Beyond the Oil Horizon: Policies Toward Sustainable Growth, edited by Ahsan Mansur and Volker Treichel. 1999.

184. Growth Experience in Transition Countries, 1990–98, by Oleh Havrylyshyn, Thomas Wolf, Julian Berengaut, Marta Castello-Branco, Ron van Rooden, and Valerie Mercer-Blackman. 1999.

183. Economic Reforms in Kazakhstan, Kyrgyz Republic, Tajikistan, Turkmenistan, and Uzbekistan, by Emine Gürgen, Harry Snoek, Jon Craig, Jimmy McHugh, Ivailo Izvorski, and Ron van Rooden. 1999.

182. Tax Reform in the Baltics, Russia, and Other Countries of the Former Soviet Union, by a staff team led by Liam Ebrill and Oleh Havrylyshyn. 1999.

181. The Netherlands: Transforming a Market Economy, by C. Maxwell Watson, Bas B. Bakker, Jan Kees Martijn, and Ioannis Halikias. 1999.

180. Revenue Implications of Trade Liberalization, by Liam Ebrill, Janet Stotsky, and Reint Gropp. 1999.

179. Disinflation in Transition: 1993–97, by Carlo Cottarelli and Peter Doyle. 1999.

178. IMF-Supported Programs in Indonesia, Korea, and Thailand: A Preliminary Assessment, by Timothy Lane, Atish Ghosh, Javier Hamann, Steven Phillips, Marianne Schulze-Ghattas, and Tsidi Tsikata. 1999.

Note: For information on the titles and availability of Occasional Papers not listed, please consult the IMF's Publications Catalog or contact IMF Publication Services.